THE NEW POLITICS

THE NEW
America and the End

By EDMUND STILLMAN

POLITICS

of the Postwar World

and **WILLIAM PFAFF**

Coward McCann, Inc.

GREENWOOD PRESS, PUBLISHERS
WESTPORT, CONNECTICUT

E
744
.S86
1984

Library of Congress Cataloging in Publication Data

Stillman, Edmund O.
    The new politics.

      Reprint. Originally published: New York : Coward-
McCann, c1961.
      Bibliography: p.
      Includes index.
      1. United States--Foreign relations--1945-   .
2. World politics--1945-   . I. Pfaff, William,
1928-   . II. Title.
E744.S86 1984   327.73   84-12756
ISBN 0-313-24383-2 (lib. bdg.)

Material from this book appeared, in somewhat different form, in HARPER'S
MAGAZINE

    The lines from "Burnt Norton" in FOUR QUARTERS, *Copyright © 1943, by
T. S. Eliot. Reprinted by permission of Harcourt, Brace & World, Inc.*

    The lines from "Connoisseur of Chaos" are reprinted from THE COLLECTED
POEMS OF WALLACE STEVENS *with the permission of the publisher Alfred A.
Knopf, Inc. Copyright © 1942, 1954 by Wallace Stevens.*

    The passage from THE ANATOMY OF REVOLUTION *by Crane Brinton reprinted
with the permission of the publisher Prentice-Hall, Inc. Copyright © 1952 by
Prentice-Hall, Inc.*

    The passage from UNITY *by* GENERAL CHARLES DE GAULLE *Copyright ©
1959 by Simon and Schuster, Inc. is reprinted by permission of the publisher.*

Reprinted in 1984 by Greenwood Press
A division of Congressional Information Service, Inc.
88 Post Road West, Westport, Connecticut 06881

Printed in the United States of America

10 9 8 7 6 5 4 3 2 1

ACKNOWLEDGMENTS

The authors wish to acknowledge their debt to the many friends and colleagues with whom these arguments have long been discussed. Their comments, objections, encouragement—all have contributed to what appears in these pages. A special note of thanks is due to Konrad Kellen, who read and commented upon the work while it was in proof, and to Marilynne Moynihan. And our gratitude—and a dedication—belong to Mary Stillman, who sustained the alliance.

❉   ❉   ❉

CONTENTS

PART ONE

The World Since the War

CHAPTER ONE

The United States and the Crisis of Policy

Here is a place of disaffection
Time before and time after
In a dim light: neither daylight
Investing form with lucid stillness
Turning shadow into transient beauty
With slow rotation suggesting permanence
Nor darkness to purify the soul
Emptying the sensual with deprivation
Cleansing affection from the temporal.

—T. S. Eliot

THE POLICY of a nation expresses its quality—we begin with this. Quality we understand as a measure not only of excellence but of character and significance. Foreign policy is both deliberate and intuitive, and no matter how coldly a plan is formulated it cannot, like mathematics, remain pure. It is a growth; place and climate, accident and thrust—and consciousness—make it what it becomes. So to talk about a policy is to talk about a society and about that difficult consensus of popular and professional intelligence and intuition which gives a nation wisdom—if it is to have wisdom.

That the policy of the United States is defective is today a truism. That it is defective despite the energy and generosity which the American nation has invested in it is a fact which is at the center of that dismay, that malaise, clearly evident in the United States in these first years of the 1960's.

11

For we have not lacked a nobility of intention in these years
of Cold War. Fifteen years now we have devoted to the Soviet
challenge and to the asserting and shaping of an American
place in the affairs of nations. We have invested deaths and
suffering in this, our material resources in unprecedented quan-
tities, and our intellectual and professional talents on a scale
equaled only in the years of war against Nazi Germany and
Imperial Japan.

Yet we are failing. Like Ezra Pound's guardsman by the north
gate we may ask what brought this to pass, "A gracious spring,
turned to blood-ravenous autumn, a turmoil of wars-men. . . ." [1]
Our policies are failing and our influence in the world is shrinking. Our European allies doubt our prudence and our will; the
new nations of the Southern Hemisphere are increasingly indifferent to our claims—when they do not despise them. Our
enemies treat us with a rough contempt; and among us there is
a sense of futility, of vain effort, and of problems—once seemingly so simple—that now elude the very categories of thought
and political discourse by which we seek solutions.

The origins of our futility defy easy analysis; in such a search-
ing our national style serves us badly. For the truths about our
failures must be sought beyond that mere level of technique
where our debates are habitually conducted. Yet we hesitate to
search deeply, for if we did, that could involve questioning the
meaning of a whole period of our national life—our period, we
like to say, of coming to maturity, of greatness in the world.

But what is the national greatness we claim? Not mere size,
surely, though we are enamored of size, nor the raw power we
wield in the world. We recognized as much in 1945 when *imperium* in the classic sense might have been ours and we made
the great refusal—indeed, when we refused even to admit the
temptation to world domination at all. (Though this temptation,
as we learned in the years that followed, is subtle and does not
always present itself as a single dramatic choice; there is a return of the repressed.)

Nor is greatness the accident of riches, or the transient leadership which may be granted a nation by a period of technological progress in which eventually all nations share. Greatness can lie in the arts and scholarship, the pure sciences; but although we have vigor and originality in these things, and in certain literary forms and in contemporary painting and architecture dominate the artistic imagination of the decade, we do not even pretend to that decisive kind of artistic and intellectual accomplishment that defines an age—as Elizabethan England was defined, or fifth-century Greece.

America's claim to greatness has always been a political claim, rooted in our Revolution and sustained by our real success in making a democratic society. It is an enduring accomplishment; we are a heterogeneous, complex, and populous state spanning a continent, where the essential elements of democracy are professed without serious challenge, the right to resist bad government legally guaranteed to the governed, the personnel of government regularly accountable to the governed. This much is a licit claim to greatness, though not a unique one.

And it antedates America's vast international involvement of the late 1940's and 1950's—the events of the time which provide us with what we have regarded as our age of greatness on the world arena. And here, despite our confident claims, our boasting, we have tasted bitterness and defeat. Our splendid isolation ended, we find our reputation and value to the world diminished. We find that involvement—the kind of involvement we have undertaken—corrodes like the sea; and we have found that we possess the terrible power to corrupt our fellows and diminish them.

This book is an examination of American foreign policy in the years since World War II. It deals with our rivalry with Russia and its allies, and the future of that rivalry, so far as that future can be foreseen. But inevitably it is a comment on American society and the national assumptions that have made our society what it is. For it is no accident that America chose to be an isolated nation for nearly a hundred and fifty years, nor that our involvement, when it came, was both generous and evangelical, both innocent and arrogant.

The American national mood, our political consciousness of ourselves, has perceptibly changed in these recent years, and not altogether for the better. But there is a constant at the center of our awareness of ourselves: a moral isolation, a reluctance to accept the demands implicit in reality, a refusal to accept our complicity in history.

Our Revolution was a curious combination of Calvinist pessimism and Enlightenment optimism. The Constitution itself was surely no optimistic document. As Richard Hofstadter has written:

> The men who drew up the Constitution in Philadelphia during the summer of 1787 had a vivid Calvinistic sense of human evil and damnation and believed with Hobbes that men are selfish and contentious. . . . They did not believe in man, but they did believe in the power of a good political constitution to control him.[2]

They provided a system by which contending interests would check the excesses of one another; in Jefferson's words, "as that no one could transcend their legal limits without being effectually checked and restrained by the others."[3]

Yet despite this acute consciousness of human limitation and perverseness, the very creation of the United States Constitution was an act of optimism. From the start, the citizens of the new nation felt themselves to be men of a new dispensation, the citizens of a new Jerusalem freed from the weight of old Europe. As Reinhold Niebuhr put it:

> We had renounced . . . the evils of European religious bigotry. We had found broad spaces for the satisfaction of human desires in place of the crowded Europe. Whether, as in the case of the New England theocrats, our forefathers thought of our "experiment" as primarily the creation of a new and purer church, or, as in the case of Jefferson and his coterie, they thought primarily of a new political community, they believed in either case that we had been called out by God to create a new humanity. We were God's "American Israel."[4]

This duality has persisted through our history. In our transition from the agrarian society of the Revolution to the intense industrial civilization of the present we have been persistently and triumphantly pragmatic in our domestic politics. Ideological parties and ideological political movements have always broken themselves on our incorrigible sense of the practical, our compromises, our mistrust of *programs* in the European sense, our intuition of the importance of individuality and dissent.

Our other face—our progressivism—has given us not only our domestic reform movement but our ambivalent relationship with the world at large. We have intervened in world affairs only three times in our history, each time with a moral zeal to put things right. Internationally the Yankee skepticism has deserted us; we have been enthusiasts. We have been hostile to the very limitation and inconstancy of humanity which our domestic politics so effectively acknowledges.

We entered the first World War to destroy Imperial Germany and remake Europe on a better pattern. It was a puritan crusade, and even more so was our role in the second World War. We were Cromwells, the sword of God. Seeing our cause as pre-eminently moral, we would admit no compromises. And admitting no compromises, we would accept no restraints.

Here is our flaw: a defective sense of history, a refusal to acknowledge our implication in time. For whatever we think, history *is* flawed and uncertain and incalculable. And if the American nation makes it its mission to solve history's riddle and bring time to a stop, it will wreck itself. That is what we are in danger of doing today.

The third of our interventions in history, the Cold War, was undertaken by the United States with a sobriety and realism that had not been present in our earlier incursions into world affairs. But here too, as the years of frustration have accrued, we have veered into messianism, into an understanding of politics as crusade—as a moral undertaking directed to a morally conceived end.

The American political intelligence has always been troubled by this relationship between morality and politics. Out of a Protestant ethical heritage, it has been reluctant to recognize the demands of the political order as being in any way different from the demands made upon the individual by the moral conscience. And as the individual was denied a selfish use of power and commanded to altruism and gentleness, the state too was made subject to these demands—despite the fact that the state manifestly lives by an ordered use of power, by a selfish concern for survival, and on occasion by mass violence. The contradictions in this outlook were never satisfactorily reconciled, but so long as America was withdrawn from international affairs the issue was evaded.

And though in contemporary Protestant thought the influence of this older and simple ethic has been reduced, it persists as an enduring element in what might be called the national unconscious. Our addiction to the word "crusade" in politics, our insistence upon defining political struggles in moral terms, are fundamental to the national political style.

While the sources of the style are Protestant, it must be understood that it exists today quite apart from Protestantism. Indeed, contemporary Protestant thought, like Catholicism with its adherence to a definition of the state as subject to moral imperatives which are not identical with those of the individual conscience, is far more "realistic" in its political philosophy than the secular politicians tend to be.

For in a certain and significant measure America has substituted politics for religion as the means for human fulfillment and transcendence. Our international politics are understood as making a world in which the ills of history will have been cured and a literally inhuman order and tranquillity will prevail. All will enjoy the advantages now exclusively American; conflict will have been conquered and strife succumb to altruism.

Young men are today commended to the Foreign Service as they once were commended to the ministry. That energy which once drove our frontier westward to the Pacific is turned into a new international quest. But while men went West to find their private destinies, to satisfy the obscure and characteristic American longing for private independence, for a new stake in new land, for a place where the past is forgotten and every man makes what he wants of himself, the idealism today is no longer individualistic but philanthropic: we are making others into something new. As Russell Davenport and the editors of *Fortune* expressed it: "We seek ways to be creative and constructive, ways in which we feel we are extending the American Proposition to other peoples." [5]

This contemporary impulse was even more precisely stated in the debate on national purpose which appeared in the press in mid-1960. Clinton Rossiter said:

We are called upon by history to guide the world, not to dominate it. And while we continue to cherish the fond belief that our country is a peculiar treasure, let us perceive that it is just such a country that may rise above its apparent self-interest in a grand attempt to secure the interest of humanity.

And Archibald MacLeish declared the American national purpose to be "to set men free." *All* men, he emphasized. [6]

But are these sentiments, distinguished as they are for altruism and generosity, the proper terms by which a political policy may be defined? Can a foreign policy be constructed to secure such transcendent ambitions—secure them not only for one nation but for mankind itself? Or do these ambitions surpass the competence of a foreign policy, and so damage it by warping it from its true accomplishment? Are these ambitions which would break the bonds of history?

It is sometimes thought a betrayal of idealism or moral purpose to insist on the limitations of politics. But it is not. It is a service—to idealism as well as to politics. Idealism carries within it the seeds of vanity and pharisaism; its vice is megalomania, whereas its true accomplishment is usually attended by a certain humility, a deference to the ambiguities of success and failure. "Time hath, my lord, a wallet at his back," said Shakespeare's Ulysses, "wherein he puts alms for oblivion, a great-siz'd monster of ingratitudes."

It is the argument of this book that the American nation has lost its way. It is failing. But it need not fail. There is a way out—though it is not the way of surrogate empire or evangelical politics. As a nation we will need wisdom. A way to begin is to look back on the years since the end of the second World War.

CHAPTER TWO

Cold War and Containment

Mr. Roosevelt's conception seemed to me an imposing one although disquieting for Europe and for France. It was true that the isolationism of the United States was . . . a great error now ended. But passing from one extreme to the other, it was a permanent system of intervention that he intended to institute by international law.

—*Charles de Gaulle*

THE COLD WAR is now familiar as a possession, its terrors banal. Its terms are so much a part of our national habit as to make the years between the surrender of Japan and the promulgation of the doctrine of containment in July 1947 a suppressed passion, an experience we remember with effort and no little pain. The Japanese surrender was to have brought release to a taut and triumphant America. The peace was to have been organized. Japan and Germany would be guarded, their victims restored, and a new world organization constructed. It was the American conviction that we stood at the threshold of the Peaceable Kingdom—there would be no more horror.

To expect then that Americans could have concerned themselves with the ominous encroachment of Soviet power in Eastern Europe would have been too much; no people in those months could have summoned the strength to imagine the implications of what then was happening in Lublin and Bucharest. The Western leaders who spoke concern over Soviet actions were ignored when they were not calumniated, for their warnings had the suspicious ring of the divisive propaganda of the Germans, against which we had spent four years on guard.

It was not only that the emotions of war were spent; it was the time of optimism's zenith. While we had progressed beyond the egregious naïveté of those Americans who in 1918 fought to end war, even the most sober in this country saw the future as a concert of nations allied to prevent a repetition of the catastrophe just experienced, reconciling their disputes with reason. Reinhold Niebuhr in 1944 had seen world community as "man's final necessity and possibility, but also his final impossibility . . . in actuality the perpetual problem as well as the constant fulfillment of human hopes." [1] But few so qualified their expectations, or were as attentive to man's darker talent as to his dream.

Europe's mood was different. People there were sated with destruction and demoralized by the reversion to barbarism which had taken place in their midst. The experience of Nazism made equally intolerable to many of them the prospect of more war, or of a return to the discredited bourgeois democracy of the 1930's—to the nationalism and narrow competition which had produced economic catastrophe, political madness in Germany, and the impotence in the face of Nazism which had marked the governments of Europe before 1939. An age clearly had ended.

In much of intellectual Europe there was a failure of confidence in Europe's civilization itself; it seemed wasted. To the disillusioned, conscious of the ruin of old pretensions, preoccupied with a philosophy which exalted the absurd, the Americans seemed to offer naïve strength but little more. Were they not a European offshoot, preserved only by geography from knowing the truth? Russia by contrast appeared a post-European civilization, unbeautiful but purged of fatuity, the pitiless successor to a West which was finished.

Europe in 1945 and 1946 brooded over its ruins, freed but exhausted, withdrawn—but finding, all unknown, renewal in the sources it had come to despise.

"Rarely can hostility have been so predictable," said Raymond Aron of the breakup of the wartime alliance between the Western democracies and the Russians. "The Germans never ceased to proclaim [the hostility between Russia and the West] . . . and Goebbels was unable to understand that the more he insisted the more he forced the Americans to camouflage it. Not for a moment, of course, did the Russian authorities forget, but the Anglo-Saxons, and particularly the Americans, often acted as if they did not regard the hostility as fundamental." [2]

Rarely can hostility have been so predictable—but rarely have people been willing to acknowledge so bitter a prediction. Both East and West lived in fantasy, though not to be sure the same fantasy: the truth about the emerging struggle was resisted with neurotic strength. If there is evidence that the Soviets, isolated for a generation and living by ideology, genuinely expected revolution to sweep postwar Europe, their awakening from fiction was quicker than the West's. Whatever their ideological illusions, the Russians never lost their feel for the reality of power, and their military possibilities in the last months of the war were exploited to the utmost. The subsequent failure of their revolutionary expectations made it clear to them that there was little else that merited reliance. Stalin, as Louis Halle has said, accepted the fact that a fundamental Communist prediction—spontaneous revolution in the war-disrupted states—had proved unreal.

If the masses would not respond to the Communist leadership of their own accord, then they would have to be conquered. The unexpectedly overwhelming defeat of the Communists in the Austrian election of 1945, and the failures of Communist subversion in Italy and France during the winter of 1947-48, must have helped teach a lesson that had already been implicit in the Russo-Finnish War of 1939.[3]

By 1946 Stalin had abandoned the ideological line of Great Power unity. His lieutenant, Zhdanov, confirmed a new hard line in November with a speech couched in the language of world dichotomy: a democratic group of states led by the Soviet Union was confronted by "reactionary circles" in Britain and America. The Cominform was established the following year, and from then on all outside the Soviet bloc was enemy.

The West's disillusionment was more gradual and provoked a deeper intellectual and moral crisis; only repeated shocks could draw us from our fantasy. The shocks were provided in gratuitous plenty; they had begun even before Germany's collapse. The Red Army acquiesced in the Warsaw massacre. Then the government of the Lublin Committee was imposed on grievously wounded Poland; in the following months the Soviets menacingly insisted upon dominating all the new governments of Eastern Europe. Their troops remained in Azerbaidjan until mid-1946, when the implicit threat of American intervention, backed by nuclear arms, proved effective to force their withdrawal. Winston Churchill declared in March 1946 that an Iron Curtain had descended upon Europe, coining a phrase that has dominated our imaginations since; but the delineation of the border between Communist control and the West was still incomplete. Civil war broke out in Greece that fall, ending even those fictions of East-West co-operation that had persisted until then.

The moral crisis was surmounted in the United States in 1947. In March of that year, when Britain declared that it could no longer sustain the Greek government against the Communist rebels, President Truman announced that the United States would give support to both Greece and Turkey (the latter had been subjected to Soviet territorial threats). In June, Secretary of State George Marshall urged that the United States "do whatever it is able to do" to restore the world's economic health, "without which there can be no political strength and no assured peace." The United States responded; it created the Marshall Plan which together with the Truman Doctrine expressed the new policy that had been adopted by the American government. That age had begun which is still with us today.

America had gone forth in 1941 to save Europe from itself. We might have sought then to return to our old isolation or taken refuge in dreams of a federated world. But we proved in the end to have the strength to see, not without anguish, that these evasions were unreal and unworthy of a great nation, and in the late 1940's we steadied to a policy that provided neither easy heroism nor early victory. There was messianism in our postwar consciousness, a sense of assuming the burden of destiny as a chosen people; but containment as formulated in the spring of 1947 was the soberest foreign policy the American people ever undertook. Promising ourselves the least glory, we won the most permanent honor.

The crucial statement of containment was provided by George Kennan with his (then anonymous) essay, "The Sources of Soviet Conduct." [4] It created an international sensation when it was published in July 1947. In retrospect it is difficult to account for the passionate terms in which Mr. Kennan's arguments were debated. So far as they were an explanation of Soviet actions in the early postwar years, his theories were sound and his practical recommendations were hardly ill-founded or rash. But we forget the world of 1947, the wracking debate over the true nature of Soviet intentions, the agony which the recognition of Soviet-American rivalry cost us, an agony evidenced ever since by the fixity with which America has clung to this theory framed in the dramatic but transient circumstances of the early postwar years. For 1947 was still a year short of an American Presidential campaign when illusion about the Soviets was pervasive enough for the Communist-manipulated Progressive Party to poll more than a million votes for its national candidates.

Containment—the term taken from one of Mr. Kennan's sentences—was to become one of those chemical elements which periodically catalyze American political debate. Indeed the dispute which followed publication of the essay more often than not had little real connection with its arguments or the related steps taken by the American government in Greece and Turkey. The American style of political debate is so frequently a matter of dealing in hypotheticals, of symbol manipulation, that only the term "emotional discourse" will accurately apply. On the political Left, in the months that followed the Truman Doctrine and during the Progressive Party campaign of 1948, containment was sometimes spoken of as virtual aggression against the Soviet Union. On the Right, particularly during the tormented months of an inconclusive Korean War and the Presidential campaign of 1952, containment was denounced as "static," a "soft" doctrine, veering close to treasonous surrender.

That it was neither ought to have been apparent. But the controversy sprang from the fact that containment provided an issue by which a far deeper American political conflict could be expressed. The specific strategy of containment became a sign of the whole issue of isolationism versus internationalism, between the self-conscious European attachments and identification of a part of America and the profound if unthinking national tradition of rejecting Europe. It was a debate which had continued in this country at least since Wilson's time. It was in considerable measure a debate of styles rather than of substance, for the incorrigible American utopianism marked much of what was felt and said on both sides. While the internationalists included men who, like Kennan and many of his colleagues in the administration of the time, had come to terms with the ambiguity of history, the popular supporters of their position often expressed the characteristic national determination to rectify time and bring the warring world to a political haven. The isolationists had a less grandiose vision, but for all that an evangelical one too: they would make America a perfected society and so by moral force—which, in Péguy's phrase, has clean hands because it has no hands—remake the world.

The battle was won by the internationalists, but at a cost. When it was over, there was tacit agreement that certain issues were settled and were not to be reopened. A national consensus had been arrived at, and our struggle with the Soviets was admitted to involve foreign economic aid, co-operation with international organizations, and military involvement throughout the world. This was our *bi-partisan* foreign policy, not to be attacked in principle. And while consensus did not mean unqualified conviction and there were times when we doubted the road we had set upon, while some in our political life were unreconciled, all the more reason then to suppress our qualms. There could be no turning back. Nor, in a deep sense, were we emotionally able to tolerate questioning of our commitment to internationalism. That would mean questioning all the agony we had been through between 1939 and 1947, and we dared not think of that again.

Yet containment itself, as formulated by George Kennan, was no more nor less than a limited and specific interpretation of Soviet ideology and society from which certain strategic conclusions could be drawn.

[Soviet] political action is a fluid stream which moves constantly, wherever it is permitted to move, toward a given goal. Its main concern is to make sure that it has filled every nook and cranny available to it in the basin of world power. But if it finds unassailable barriers in its path, it accepts these philosophically and accommodates itself to them. The main thing is that there should always be pressure, unceasing constant pressure, toward the desired goal.[5]

It was the purpose of containment, a defensive strategy though one from which a meaningful tactic could be developed, to frustrate this Soviet expansion and, by so doing, to intensify the internal strains of Soviet society. Kennan's was a conservative program, reflecting a sober turn of mind little in sympathy with the extremes of zeal and sentimentality in American political life. He offered a program of "adroit and vigilant application of counterforce at a series of constantly shifting geographical and political points, corresponding to the shifts and manoeuvres of Soviet policy." He saw Soviet intentions as determined by a warped ideological inheritance and a thirty-year history of implacable and unscrupulous hostility to all not of their camp—a projection of their own fears and misery. He saw Russian society worn by deprivation, terror, and war, barren of real ideas. He saw the older generation destroyed as an intellectual force and the new generation as an unknown. He saw Soviet economic progress as sporadic and unbalanced, the nation "economically ... vulnerable, and in a certain sense ... impotent. ... capable of exporting its enthusiasms and of radiating the strange charm of its primitive political vitality but unable to back up those articles of export by the real evidences of material power and prosperity."

"The future of Soviet power," he argued, "may not be by any means as secure as Russian capacity for self-delusion would make it appear to the men in the Kremlin. ... If ... anything were ever to occur to disrupt the unity and efficacy of the Party as a political instrument, Soviet Russia might be changed overnight from one of the strongest to one of the weakest and most pitiable of national societies." To Kennan, as to most observers of the Soviet Union in 1947, the question of power succession appeared the flaw most likely to shatter the convoluted apparatus of totalitarian control.

Thus containment, as formulated in 1946-1947, was a policy rooted in a series of definite assumptions about the nature of Soviet reality. They were reasonable, perhaps inspired assumptions. The policy was not one of vast muddling through— a political Micawberism founded in the easy and vain expectation that something would turn up. It recommended actions that would exploit the weaknesses it perceived in the Soviet system while blunting the Soviet strengths.

More important, it was a policy directed to a defined goal. At some critical moment the besieged giant would weaken: his ambitions and powers would be dulled, he would turn upon himself in frenzy or in melancholy. Kennan chose a comparison

with the Buddenbrooks in Thomas Mann's novel: "Human institutions often show the greatest outward brilliance at a
moment when inner decay is in reality farthest advanced...."

But the prophecy failed. Like families, societies may have
incalculable powers of renewal, and in the years after 1947
Russia proved itself tougher and more resourceful than we
had thought.

Of the events which Kennan foresaw and upon which he
predicated his policy, some have come and gone, and been ignored; and some seem unlikely ever to come. Yet while the
architect of the containment policy has revised much in his
own position during the years that have followed, the United
States Government, under Republicans as under Democrats,
has been implacably faithful—in its fashion—to the program
stated in that seminal but now wholly unread article in *Foreign
Affairs* published in what seems another age.

And during those years the realities of Soviet society have
been transformed. The context in which the ideology functions
is not at all what it was in 1947, nor is the ideology itself un-
touched. Khrushchev has invoked Lenin himself against those
who resist the recasting of Leninist arguments. The Russia of
today is not the stricken early industrial society it was at the
war's end; the economy remains unbalanced, to be sure, but in
those basic areas which fortify its military and political claims
the Soviet Union is a formidable power and continues to grow
at rates which a decade ago would have seemed preposterous.
Sputnik, Lunik, and the ICBM have been launched. What
"evidences of material power" could be more real? Nor is the
economy so Spartan as it used to be. By the standards of
Western Europe and North America, life for the Russian remains hard and unrewarding, but by the standards of Russia's
recent past it is not a bad life, and for the first time in a
generation there is reason for the individual Russian to feel a
sense of economic progress and an expectation that the
future will be better.

Indeed, materialism has taken its revenge: Communism's ideology is exported still, but buttressed by the commonplace recommendation to foreigners that it will make them efficient and prosperous. The homely and gnomic Khrushchev seems more concerned with the awkward reconciling of the old beliefs with new facts than he is with relighting the Bolshevik zeal of the 1920's. For the prediction Kennan made in 1947 is exactly reversed: evidences of material prosperity Russia can adduce aplenty; it is the "primitive political vitality" that is gone. It will not be recaptured. The foreign pilgrims go no longer to Moscow as to the new Jerusalem; they go to learn engineering, not philosophy.

In 1947 the Soviet Union dominated Europe from the Baltic to the Aegean; its outposts were in Vienna and on the Elbe. Moscow had not adventured so far into the West since 1814, when Russian armies, triumphant on the Seine, stood revealed to Europe, as Arthur Bryant has said, as a kind of "force of the future. It seemed a strange thing . . . to see 'a Bashkir Tartar with the Phrygian cap and bow' gazing about him from his ragged horse in a Paris street. The inscrutable, smiling barbarism of Russia both fascinated and repelled the West." [6] One hundred thirty-three years later the West European response was not so different. This quasi-Tartar hero seemed indeed the future, and all the states of East-Central Europe save Czechoslovakia were ruled by Party janissaries and dominated by the Red Army. The eastern portions of Germany and Austria were occupied, and Czechoslovakia itself—that brief nation which had seemed the beginning and the end of all that inter-wars liberalism had meant—was buckling under the pressure of its domestic Communism and Soviet diplomacy: the purpose of both was to enfeeble and destroy a government which, with a deadly earnestness born of desperation, saw its role as a bridge between East and West, a reconciler of irreconcilables. The Communist *coup d'état* of February 1948 put an end to that dream, eradicating the last salient of Western liberalism from a region marked out by the Soviets as their own.

By the early 1950's, with Yugoslavia expelled from the Cominform for nationalist heresy and the Greek Civil war ended, the line of demarcation between areas of control in Europe was fixed. The threat Communism now posed to Western Europe was military, not political; the governments of France, Italy, and the Lowlands were secure. Marshall Aid and the Anglo-American military guarantees provided for in the North Atlantic Treaty of 1949 had underwritten Europe's economic and political recovery. Communism had successfully been contained within the areas Soviet troops had controlled or screened at the close of the second World War. The Soviet conquests stood revealed for what they were in fact—military conquests.

In Asia, the mainland war had been a triangular affair and the defeat of Japan had left two native powers struggling for mastery in China. Russia's Asian role in 1945 was ambiguous, handing over to the Chinese Communists a large part of the military equipment taken from the Japanese armies in Manchuria, but also acknowledging the Kuomintang government and successfully laying claim to restoration of Russian imperial privileges in Port Arthur and Dairen—unpopular demands hardly bespeaking Soviet confidence in the outcome of the Communists' struggle with the Kuomintang.

In fact the Chinese Communists did succeed—with little help from anyone. Sweeping through China between 1946 and 1949, they established themselves as not only the most populous Communist nation in the world, but as a Communist state implicitly senior in its claims, even from the beginning, to all but Russia itself; its leader, Mao Tse-tung, ranking as theorist and innovator next to Lenin and Stalin. For the future, who could tell? It was no satellite that was established in Peking; it was a state which the world rightly looked upon with apprehension. It represented an enormous acquisition of strength for Communism, but with a difference: it was a second center of power and ideology. Mao Tse-tung and Chou En-lai were not imperial proconsuls, dependent upon Moscow for support as they imposed hated policies on a vanquished people. They were leaders in a very old Chinese tradition, masters of their own conquests, and the homage they paid to Moscow was deferential and fraternal, but unobsequious.

Very early, and rightly so, the postwar administration in America saw the issue of Communism in China as different in kind from the Soviet conquest of Eastern Europe. In its estimate of Chinese Communist intentions it may have been naïve; but it perceived the Communist victory as a victory in civil war—a war in which a foreign state could intervene only with supreme difficulty. Containment of Communism was never seriously attempted by the United States in Asia until after 1950. The doctrine of containment was originated in the context of European developments and the Russian threat; moreover, there seemed no apparent way in which suppression of the Chinese Communists could be accomplished without a massive American military intervention, and that was unthinkable. So having no clear opportunity to exert a decisive influence on China, yet profoundly concerned over what was happening, the United States did what nations usually do in such circumstances: too much and too little. It ineffectually supported the ineffectual Kuomintang, thereby implicating itself in its defeat. It muddled about, consoling itself with its obstinate illusions about the Chinese and their reputed gratitude for the traditional anticolonialist role played in mainland affairs by the United States. The Communists in fact had no such affecting memories of the unrequited American fascination with China. America became, and has ever since remained, the focus of China's renewed and officially sponsored xenophobia—the outer barbarians, the "paper tiger" ejected from the mainland in 1949, to be "defeated" again in Korea.

By 1952, when the Korean War had ended in a stalemate, the line of containment throughout the world had implicitly been acknowledged by both the Communists and the Western powers. In accordance with the Kennan thesis of damming the flow of Communist power, the Western allies had fought in Greece, had met military pressure with counterpressure in Turkey, had chosen to sustain Berlin by airlift during the blockade, and in Korea in 1950 had gone to war against a Communist intrusion. The Soviet Union and China (the latter most dramatically with its intervention on the Yalu) had made equally plain their unwillingness to tolerate any Western attempt to reclaim territories within the line of military demarcation. It was containment, but mutual containment, and it presumed essentially military terms.

The tactical development of the containment strategy had taken place in the Europe of the late 1940's. There the crisis was familiar in shape, the remedies required were unprecedented in scale but of a recognizable design. Europe had needed economic reconstruction, and America provided generous capital funds. But the economy being rebuilt was the one which had dominated the world for three centuries, a subtle and resourceful system functioning in a culture of great sophistication. The political alliance was established in equally congenial conditions: the Europe which had found solidarity in resisting Nazi Germany maintained that solidarity in the face of the new danger, and eventually brought the restored Germany into partnership. The Christian Democrats and Socialists who shaped postwar Europe were internationalists concerned with making a new Europe—perhaps a federated Europe. NATO was to be followed by a coal and steel community, a continental nuclear authority, and an economic alliance. Overshadowed by Russia and America in the postwar years, Europeans found in their tradition and history their common cause and quite deliberately set out to give a new political expression to their community. Britain and America, different, yet closer to Europe in their politics and culture than to any but their own Atlantic and Commonwealth community, joined themselves to the Continent in making a political alliance more meaningful and extensive than any in history. The manifest thrust of Soviet aggression and America's initiatives had coincided with an authentic European impulse toward unity, and the Atlantic Alliance was a triumph.

It was the most brilliant achievement of the policy of containment. And it was, for all its success, to blight American policy during the years that have followed. For after the European success, American policy became a ritual invocation of the European formula—in circumstances where it could not and did not work. This tactic of military treaty and military-economic aid was raised to the level of a world strategy. The United States was set upon the task of ringing Russia with alliances. It sought military bases, but after the Korean War it carried out this military project in a political context increasingly divorced from the realities of a changing world.

As the challenges to the West multiplied, and the contest with the Communists spilled over from the European theater into Asia, with China entering the lists on Russia's side, the United States was compelled to commit itself on a whole series of new fronts. In 1947 the proposition that America would soon be fighting a ground war in Korea would have seemed as incredible a prediction as that still later we would find ourselves in a shrill dispute with Russia over the destinies of Cuba. In the 1940's our policies were still directed to the containment of Soviet and Chinese *military* power; we had not yet seen our struggle as one for the allegiance of mankind itself. A Presidential proposal for a world referendum on the issue of Communism versus the American political system would in 1947 have seemed implausible if not impertinent. In 1960, when it was in fact made, it seemed hardly remarkable: the revolution in America's thinking during the decade was imposing.

Events dominated in those early postwar years, and the United States sought policy for the new challenges in the lessons of its European experience. It was inevitable that we did so; and the early results justified the decision. Economic support was provided for the troubled new Asian nations. The technical assistance program adopted in 1949 supplemented modest direct aid. Our military policy in Asia was to hold the island defense line that existed at the end of the war, and we expected no military involvement on the mainland—nor indeed did we expect any military challenge in Asia at all. As for the Middle East—that, we felt, was Britain's concern more than ours.

The Korean War was the turning point in our Asia policy. For we were badly hurt in Korea, mauled and deprived of clear victory. At home the experience seared the national conscience, damaging our faith in our own invincibility, adding climax to the postwar trauma. The result was sobering, surely, forcing upon us some understanding of the necessity for inconclusive conflict; but the larger effects of Korea were damaging to America. Shaken in confidence, divided by the unexpected renewal, during Senator McCarthy's career, of an old and virulent domestic quarrel, we lost our assurance. Where before we had thought of ourselves as one of an alliance, we now felt ourselves to be alone. We were paying the cost of responsibility; our allies, we felt, were not. The menace was not, we thought, really understood by our allies. They had not contributed to the Korean War in the way we had; they had questioned our advance to the Yalu and advised compromise; they were critical and suspicious of us; they sometimes talked of an American "fascism," adopting an irresponsible and righteous manner that left us enraged and ashamed. Our domestic upheaval was ill-understood by others but for us it was a dreadfully familiar outbreak of that nativism, that neurotic nationalism, always a part of us—a contest, for better or worse, to be settled by us only and in our own time. When it was over, and the Korean War had ended, a kind of weary calm returned to America; but we were a different nation.

The America of the years that followed Korea was hurt and humorless; its foreign policy was uncompromising. If during the interval between 1945 and Korea we had made terms with the demands of history, the pain we experienced in 1951 and

1952 wrecked that accommodation. On both Left and Right there was a reversion to an older sense of national separateness, to our intolerance of time. Our messianism had always expressed itself in two forms: the expansive and liberal wish to remake the world on a better model, and a conservatism no less idealistic but fearful of involvement in the tarnished world, wishing rather to give an example to it. As the first Eisenhower administration—the first Liberal Republican administration— was, in domestic political terms, a compromise between internationalist and nationalist elements in our life, so its foreign policy was faithful to the country's mood. International involvement and responsibility were accepted, but in a new way. The drama was now pre-eminently a moral one. Now we were in a very real sense obsessed with this challenge of Communism. We talked with a new earnestness of liberating the satellites and of victory over Russia, and while these were campaign slogans and expressed no specific program, they were not hyprocrisy: they were seriously meant, and that we did not know how we would accomplish these things indicated only that we had not yet found the means to work our will.

Nor was there anything in Russian policy to encourage detachment. Nineteen-fifty to 1953 were the years of Stalinism's dreadful climax. Purges had swept Eastern Europe in 1949-50 and again in 1951-52; the "Doctor's Plot" in early 1953 recalled the horrors of the Great Purge. The Soviet Union seemed caught up in a state of paranoia, incomprehensible and dangerous, capable of any lunatic act.

Our early postwar policy had been primarily *political*— limited and pragmatic; our evangelism influenced but did not lead our actions. After Korea our outraged moral sense ruled, and we were no longer content to contain this evil; it had to be extirpated. Calvinists that as a nation we are, we saw depravity manifest in the world, and we, the elect, had to combat it. We told ourselves that this was our mission; that this was the American century, the time of our testing.

The altered temper of our policy unified the nation as our

wartime policy had unified it. We followed our old impulse to generalize our national experience to the world at large. It was a renewal of the enthusiasms of World War II, for then we had looked to a federated world, One World, with the great powers exercising a benevolent guardianship. Charles de Gaulle had termed this wartime goal "a permanent system of intervention which [America] intended to institute by international law." But the phrase was more appropriate to our post-Korean policy. Again it was permanent intervention that we undertook: for swept up by a sense of great ethical issues and great events, feeling ourselves alone in our perception of the almost Manichean scale of this struggle, we came to sense that all depended on us. We had no time for those who could not understand this imposing but exhilarating destiny that was ours.

The outline of our post-Korean strategy was simple enough; we would invest the enemy, extending to Asia the wall of defense that we had begun in Europe. Siege was a plan very much within our tradition of maritime strategy. True enough, it committed us on external lines, while Russia and China enjoyed the advantages of internal lines, but we have always conducted overseas campaigns and preferred blockade. Where we departed from all our strategic traditions was in surrendering mobility. Though we did not see it then, we had adopted a political program analogous to France's committing all its forces in 1939 to the Maginot Line, or as though Britain had fought Napoleon not on the sea and by probes in Spain and the Lowlands, but by static land warfare in Central Europe.

The strategy of extended siege seemed to us a logical development of George Kennan's earlier interpretation of Soviet prospects, but it was not. Kennan had called, not for siegeworks, but for the adroit application of force at constantly shifting points to counter the Soviet sallies. And even his reading of Soviet reality was by 1953 made obsolete by Stalin's death and the far-ranging economic and political alterations that followed in Russia.

The siege strategy was to become irrelevant before it was really begun, although we clung to the notion with the fixity of men to whom ideas come seldom, and then as an agony. The discrepancy between the real Soviet threat and the measures we undertook to contain it steadily widened. The Communist bloc under Stalin had given the West every legitimate reason to fear attack. Within a year of Stalin's death, however, the New Course was launched and brought not only a series of political concessions and a redirection of the Soviet economy reflecting a certain reformist and defensive mood in the Kremlin, but a foreign policy which now aimed at exploiting the "internal contradictions" of capitalism through a new program of "peaceful coexistence"—of political action short of war or the proximate threat of war. The abrupt ending of Stalin's ranting hostility to all outside his rule suggested to many in the world abroad that the Soviet Union had abandoned its universalist and aggressive ambitions. That much was delusion. What did happen was that the new Russia chose to wait. Ringing blows against the non-Communist states were stopped, and political and economic influence was sought in the world to undermine the enemy's influence and prepare the way for the long-heralded inevitable revolution. The ideological interpretations of Asian nationalism and bourgeois democracy were reviewed; Nehru and Sukarno, no longer identified by Soviet polemicists as the running dogs of the imperialists, became, for the Soviets, authentic popular leaders in a stage of political development which would prove the prelude to Communism. It was, in short, a return essentially to the program of the Popular Front, and it still presumed the workings of a Marxist dialectic of history leading inexorably to a Communist world.

The important changes occurred almost simultaneously in Russia and America during the early 1950's: our evangelical sense, generous but not without arrogance, was reviving, and our policies were hardening. Soviet ambitions persisted but with an unprecedented tactical sense of the pragmatic. The contest was less military—by 1955 the last important fighting front, Indochina, had been closed down—and increasingly political. Where Stalin's Russia had denounced nationalism and neutralism, the new Russia scrupulously cultivated the friendship of the uncommitted states, and it was the United States which now accused the Indians of political immorality. America was set upon constructing an interlocking system of anti-Communist alliances that would not only surround Russia but would enlist every anti-Communist—or non-Communist—state anywhere, no matter how distant those states might be from Communist armies or how remote from the issues of world politics.

As America worked to weld this iron ring of universal containment, it fell victim to a series of deep fallacies about the relevance of the European tactic to the world at large.

When the Atlantic Alliance was put together, Europe's governments were legitimate and representative; the general public in Europe acknowledged the menace of Soviet aggression and of subversion by the militant Communist parties in their midst; they were willing to support defensive measures. The American contribution to NATO was the largest, but the Alliance nevertheless was genuine, with European initiative and will deeply committed. Europe in the late 1940's had to rebuild a war-wrecked economy, but this was the economy which had dominated the globe since the Industrial Revolution, and it was rich in resources and talent. These conditions for alliance did not exist in the states which were to be grouped in the SEATO and Baghdad alliances. The Asian nations which the United States sought to align against the Communists were young and troubled, attempting to create entirely new industrial economies out of preliterate peasant and nomadic societies. They were governed at best by narrow elites, and at worst by adventurous factions, "Herodian" converts to the West, cut off from a loyalty to the nations' past. The only political issue grasped by the public at large in these states was nationalism, and that nationalism was not so much ideological as visceral, a galvanic reaction to their colonial past. The conflicts of great powers and of European ideologies were remote and incomprehensible.

Common action with the United States for defined and limited purposes could have been meaningful for these nations, but the alliances which were created in Baghdad and Bangkok, on American initiative, were too ambitious and ill-defined to rest on a real community of purpose. Influenced by its taste for political nominalism, the United States behaved as though the signing of a treaty could manufacture that fundamental community of interest which alone makes an alliance valid. The program America was carrying out was consequently one which came to require pretense on a scale that demeaned the United States—and its allies.

We began with a quest for military bases, but before it was over we were supplying arms, economic support, and military guarantees on every continent. Having failed to examine precisely what we wanted from each of these alliances beyond a mere profession of allegiance to our cause, we gave military arrangements political warrant and justified political pacts with military arguments. Our confusion of purpose was evident in our own rhetoric. We could simultaneously speak of "using" Asians to fight Asians and of the Free World alliance without really meaning the cynicism of the former or the ingenuousness of the latter. We justified economic assistance before Congress and the American public with specious political arguments and came in time to believe our awry logic, indiscriminately applying economic assistance as a palliative to civil war in the Philippines, Arab-Israeli border skirmishes, and general Latin American discord. Yet we had every evidence, from common knowledge of the history of Europe in the last century to the most elaborate of sociological investigations in the twentieth, to tell us that economic development in a backward country leads, in the short run, to social upheaval. If the movement of industrial development is theoretically toward order, it is through disorder—the destruction of the existing political-social vessel. Economic assistance has its own value and justification; to have used it as the universal political remedy was as vain as it was intellectually disreputable.

More dangerously—and less honorably—American military aid was made into a kind of political currency, a talisman of . United States friendship, and it was distributed impartially— to feuding Asian republics, Latin-American dictatorships, and tribal empires in Africa. We supplied it with small regard for regional problems, the realities, even the geographical proximity, of the Sino-Soviet military threat, or the axiom that force in being has consequences as momentous as force employed. Formal restrictions were placed on the use of these gifts of arms, but promises were powerless to prevent their employment in colonial and civil wars, or to keep these weapons from upsetting local power balances and provoking senseless arms races.

This indiscriminate quest for allies aligned the United States in mutual assistance with governments composed of fractions— sometimes marginal fractions—in the affairs of their countries, and inevitably committed the United States to the fortunes of these groups. Whereas in NATO we were allied with states possessing legitimacy and authenticity, we elsewhere indulged in the illusion that our benediction could transform synthetic governments into real ones and that we were competent to nominate suitable governments for lesser states. We associated ourselves with some governments (as in Iraq, Cuba or Laos) which promptly collapsed and with some others (as in Vietnam, Korea or the Republic of China) which continued to exist only by a kind of repression which we found it convenient to ignore. We did not do this dumbly or with an easy conscience; we argued the ethics of intervention, but we intervened—measuring every event on the single scale of Communism/anti-Communism.

In short, we fell victim to the belief that we were universally responsible and universally competent; and, more dangerous still, we came secretly to love (and so to magnify) these vast responsibilities we once had abhorred. Allied to more than twoscore nations, from Italy and England to Iran and the Dominican Republic, we inexorably involved ourselves in the affairs of all, and the flavor of this power did not displease us.

Deliberate or not, it was, in de Gaulle's expression, a permanent system of intervention. If it was not, as de Gaulle also suggested, a conscious will to power, it surely expressed an American addiction to illusion. Entranced by Communism, we persistently searched for the hand of the Soviets in every remote and squalid political contretemps; we read every crisis as a move in a titanic struggle for the world. Victimized by our own sense of omnipotence, we came to attribute to the Soviets (themselves dangerously addicted to fantasy) an influence and power over world affairs which they did not possess.

The alliance tactic, invented to deal with the specific threat of military aggression in Europe, was being applied to every ill from Russia's intrusion into Iran to the labyrinthine communal quarrels of Lebanon. It was called containment, but containment of what? Not of the Soviet Union, for Russia's tactics after 1953 were to cultivate political and economic power, not to press military conquest. Their trade and diplomacy and their foreign instruments, the satellite governments and the Communist Parties abroad, were used to support anti-Western nationalist movements in Asia and Africa. The partnerships they formed with nationalist governments and factions in the Middle East and Asia ripped apart the system of alliances to which the United States had committed its prestige and in which the United States falsely believed its interests to lie.

The Baghdad Alliance was hardly more than a planning staff when Russia arranged a major arms supply from Eastern Europe to Egypt and collapsed the whole power system the West was attempting to build up in the Mediterranean. The USSR did not, to be sure, win Egypt as a satellite. It is a crucial point that all these partnerships were tactical arrangements, not Soviet conquests. The Soviet Union was no more able to control these nationalisms than was the West, and when it had attempted to do so in Asia, it had been defeated—as it was later to be rebuffed in Iraq and in Egypt. But in the mid-1950's the Soviet Union wished to spoil the Western position in the Middle East, and Egypt—ambitious, resentful of the support the West was giving to rival Iraq and Israel, anxious for arms but unwilling to join an American alliance—welcomed Russian help. Czechoslovakia provided the arms and aircraft, and Russia the diplomatic and economic support. The United States rebuked Egypt with a calculated insult on the Aswan Dam issue. Egypt retaliated by nationalizing the Suez Canal. In the chaos that ensued, the Egyptians, with their Russian allies, triumphed over Britain and France, and implicitly over the United States. Within twenty-one months Syria was a part of Egypt, Lebanon and Jordan had given up overtly pro-Western policies for forms of neutrality, and the Baghdad Alliance had lost Baghdad itself to an erratic and passionately anti-Western Arab nationalism.

Russia had gained no new lands, nor more than allies of expedience; and Russian armies surely continued to be contained. But the West had been hurt badly and was on the defensive. The siege was being lifted. The painfully wrought alliances were helpless against this new assault of nationalism supported by the resources of Russia and defended by the shield of Soviet missiles.

Nationalism was at flood in 1956. The Western powers had uncomprehendingly set themselves against this force and were being thrown aside. Russia—itself a victim of nationalism in Europe in 1956—was moving with the tide in the Middle East and Asia. The United States, which had set out to contain Communism, was now straining to contain nationalism. Indeed, for one bleak period in 1957 and 1958 it seemed set on using the Sixth Fleet to contain disorder itself—the bloody-mindedness of the world.

A suitable comment could have been found in Colonel Lawrence's description of the Arab Revolt. He had written:

How would the Turk defend [Arabia]? No doubt by a trench line across the bottom, if we came like an army with banners; but suppose we were (as we might be) an influence, an idea, a thing intangible.... We might be a vapor, blowing where we listed.... It seemed a regular soldier might be helpless without a target, owning only what he sat on....[7]

The United States had constructed a marvelous system of alliances to halt the Soviet army. But the Soviet army did not march. And like the Turk, in the night we watched the starry explosions where the guerrillas of modern politics wrecked our siegeworks.

An American enterprise—begun to contest the aggressive expansion of another state—had grotesquely grown into what we envisaged as a struggle for the world itself. A limited diplomatic policy, begun in Europe, had been transformed into a method for enlisting the world in our ranks—and was failing this grand ambition. The world had grown too complex for an American foreign policy conceived amid the fears and enthusiasms of another day.

CHAPTER THREE

The Rise of a Plural World

After all the pretty contrast of life and death
Proves that these opposite things partake of one,
At least that was the theory, when bishops' books
Resolve the world. We cannot go back to that.
The squirming facts exceed the squamous mind,
If one may say so. And yet relation appears,
A small relation expanding like the shade
Of a cloud on sand, a shape on the side of a hill.
—Wallace Stevens

IN THE DECADE and a half since the formulation of the doctrine of containment, the United States and its allies have, to an alarming degree, adopted the Marxist postulate of their struggle with Communism. The fatal dichotomy into what politicians defined as "free world" and "slave" was dumbly accepted; "balance of power" had, like those other cardinal sins of international life, "power politics" and "secret diplomacy," been put aside as obsolete.

A ravaged world consigned the concept of balance of power to limbo, for it seemed in 1945 that a tradition of hypersubtle diplomacy had led only to the near-ultimate catastrophes of the first and second World Wars. There was a measure of justice in this judgment, for the chanceries of old Europe had never abjured war as an instrument of even casual policy—else why the incredible insouciance with which the Austrians began the first World War? Thus, in the second World War, in a kind of agony of revulsion, the dream was born of a unified mankind.

It may be said that the Soviets too were caught up in a

43

vision—a kindred one. For if it was never the Soviet intention to submerge themselves in a world order in which their saline difference would be dissipated and the bland majority prevail, they too sought security in the fiction of a single world system. But the Russian impulse to a unitary system long antedated the second World War and sprang from a philosophy of dialectic made a ruling dogma by the Bolshevik revolution of 1917. And the messianic sense is an ancient component of Russian state policy: what may, perhaps, have been a new ingredient in 1945, as apologists for the Soviets are always noting, was the sense of urgency born of fear with which they sought to enlist the societies adjacent to their frontiers.

The impulse to a unitary system, both East and West, grew then from the ravages of the second World War, but the dream was easily confounded. The Western illusions about Soviet policy were destroyed by a series of aggressive Soviet thrusts into East-Central Europe, Manchuria, and the Middle East. The Soviet illusion—that they could in fact succeed in alchemizing the old societies of Europe—was shattered by the failure of revolution in France, Italy, and Greece. The spheres of postwar influence were stabilized finally, as we have seen, along the lines of military occupation at the war's end. By 1947 what had been a line of military demarcation between Soviet and Anglo-American patrols was converted into a political and social *limes* between two world systems.

In a certain sense this division of the world grew from the secession of the Soviets from the wartime grand alliance. But the American decision from 1945 to 1947 to organize an anti-Soviet system sprang from deeper causes than simple military threat. It was not only the Russians who labored under the burden of messianic conviction.

The record is clear enough. We misread the meaning of an essentially impermanent state of affairs at the war's close: dichotomy was a condition of international life in 1945, not because a Satanic state had gathered to itself the remaining forces of evil in the world and we as a nation were called to greatness to obliterate this evil. There was a dichotomy in the world, between us and the Soviets, because all but two powers had been wrecked by the blind forces of war. It was not, however, a state of affairs that could be expected to endure, though in the decade that followed, it persisted, with the United States and the Soviet Union fostering the division of the world into two centralized power systems.

To a Communist historian all this was inevitable. History has its truth, and there is no balancing it with untruth. And a Communist society is polarized, for truth admits no inconsistencies, past or present. But for the rest of the world, polarization was an abnormal condition.

The specific Western purpose in constructing an alliance was the classic need to organize mutual support. And in a sense it was not a new alliance we called into being so much as a continuation of the wartime alliance into a new phase. The break with the Soviets had left the essential machinery of co-operation intact, for the Russians, morose and secretive, had never really become allies; they had been the beneficiaries of trust. It was not even, in the first years after 1945, an *American* alliance system; the degree of loss of strength and will among our Western allies was not immediately apparent.

At the core of this alliance were the democracies of Western Europe and America. Around that nucleus came to be grouped states whose affiliation with what was essentially an Atlantic system was more by extension of courtesy than of logic and fact: there was, for example, Iraq, a nation having frontiers but only the most rudimentary sense of nationality. There was Turkey, a state which as the Ottoman Empire, the military vanguard of the Islamic world in the sixteenth and seventeenth centuries, had provided the stimulus to an earlier European grand alliance. There was, eventually, Spain, an aberrant relic of the Western past—a society essentially pre-industrial and pre-capitalist and whose government did not, in fact, merit the epithet *totalitarian* because its articulated goals, in a profound sense, antedated the rise of the modern state.

Beyond the alliance system itself, but enjoying its protection, were nations and communities more disparate still: the newly independent Asian members of the Commonwealth, the Africans who were nearing statehood, the remaining colonial possessions of Europe.

Fascinated with its role as protector of the West, the United States made a kind of counter-empire. The cumulative effect of our policies was the collection of what might be called an imperial federation: it was an empire, even if a benign one, maintained by a subtle nexus of political, economic, and status relations. For the primary members of this empire, Britain and France and ultimately West Germany, possessed a significant veto power over the actions of the federation—though they too were in the final analysis dependent upon Washington. There was a whole series of associated states without significant voice, chiefly states beyond the Atlantic system itself, where narrow elites, converts to Western society who could frame their political papers in the vocabulary of parliamentarianism and economic progress, undertook to speak for societies hardly able to grasp the reality of an outside world.

The United States and its major allies were engaged in a complicated military-economic-social response to the Soviet challenge, and the alliance system, jerry-built and inconsistent as it may have been, was a response rational enough in the context of the postwar collapse of hopes. But to have continued with this effort after the Korean stalemate, raising a tactical response to the level of dogma, was to misread what was happening—and would continue to happen—to alter the distribution of power in the world.

The fact that at the end of the second World War only two states remained with the ability to take decisive action on the international stage was an anomaly, the climax of a short-range historical trend—the decline of the Great Powers—which had begun around the turn of the century.

In 1900 the roster of great and near-great powers included

Imperial Russia, Great Britain, France, Germany, Ottoman Turkey, Austria-Hungary, the United States, and Japan. It was an era of unchallenged dominance of the European idea; yet of the eight states which could claim to be great powers, only four were, strictly speaking, European. One, Ottoman Turkey, was neither a European society (though it held extensive colonial possessions in the borderlands of Europe) nor, except by a kind of extravagant courtesy and the tacit interest of contending neighbors, was it a great power at all. It was a walking corpse; but it suited the interests of all concerned, in that secure and elaborate age, to defer to it as a fiction worth preserving.

Beyond the confines of Europe proper there were three other great powers—akin to, or derivative from, the great powers of Europe, but different in kind. Japan, in the early twentieth century, was the future unrecognized. It was an Asian, non-white state—by all the contemporary rules fair prey to the Europeans. Yet it would not defer to Europe. It had made an extraordinary transition from feudal seclusion to industrial parity: by 1900 Osaka mills were successfully challenging the primacy of Manchester, and Japan's navy was already very large in an era when armored fleets were the currency of great-power politics. Its navy was soon to destroy the Far Eastern and Baltic fleets of Imperial Russia and inflict the first significant defeat on a European or quasi-European state since the intrusion of Portuguese sea power into the Indian Ocean in the fifteenth century.

Japan was regarded as a kind of evolutionary sport. But in fact its emergence was a sign of a movement of history which we will need to discuss in greater detail below—the radiation into non-European territories of the technological and political discoveries of Europe. By a combination of circumstances— among them a plural and feudal past rather than a history of centralized bureaucratic despotism, a native culture practiced for centuries in the arts of technical and aesthetic borrowing, a homogeneous population secure in an island fortress, and the

presence of the ores and energy fuels necessary to industrialization—Japan had made the successful transition from a society
at the level of the European sixteenth century to the nineteenth
in a little over fifty years. In the later nineteenth century the
claims of Japan to a voice in the counsels of the great powers
was an embarrassment; after 1905 and the defeat of Imperial
Russia, the older powers did not quite dare to ignore its claims.

The next of the aberrant great powers was Imperial Russia, a
borderland of the West. As a nation it had interacted with
Europe for three centuries at least, but it had avoided the
Renaissance, the Reformation, and all but the most superficial
effects of the Enlightenment. Sprung from the wreck of the
Byzantine Empire, marked with the stamp of Mongol occupation in its infancy, xenophobic, particularist, passionate,
haunted by messianic convictions, Russia was in 1900 an awesome power, but simultaneously suffered a social malaise which
was to render it feeble for another quarter century. As a nation
it was a kind of uneasy convert to the West: it was eclectic, yet
in a profound sense it loathed itself for being so. It admired
Germanic efficiency, French literary models, and Italian archi-
tectural styles, yet it proclaimed a contempt for European
civilization at all levels of society, including frequently the
court—which spoke French. In part its social malaise was an
expression of the tension between its non-Western past and the
intrusive culture of the West—a culture which this neo-Byzan-
tine state was forced to import in order to compete and survive.

It was not, however, a weak state, for all the catastrophes
which lay ahead of it in the early twentieth century. It had
played a great role in the wars of Europe at a time when the
art of war did not require more than rudimentary technological skills and more than a fractional mobilization of the
resources of the state. In such circumstances it could compete—
and compete successfully—as Charles XII and Napoleon had
learned. But as the movement of industrialization and social
reform advanced in Western and Central Europe, Russia fell
steadily behind. It had remade itself in Peter the Great's day

into a model of a European absolutism; but while the seeds of commerce and industry were sprouting vigorously in the late nineteenth century, the Russian government, still caught in political theories that owed more to the seventeenth and eighteenth centuries than the nineteenth, failed to keep pace. Yet here was a vast, energetic, and patient people who were being increasingly drawn into the currents of change.

The last of these allogene great powers was the United States, a colonial offshoot of England, a plural state much like England in its institutions, but an Anglo-Saxon culture writ large. Like Russia, the United States, while nominally a conventional power, was on a continental scale, and like it had expanded into virtually uncontested border regions of the Western world. It had had successes, but essentially easy successes. Its dominant characteristics were a practical energy, a meliorist philosophy, a predilection for ethical politics, and an abiding concern with its internal affairs. Geography—the frontier, with all it meant to the American imagination—spared it the *intensity* of culture that marked Europe. It was an offshoot of old Europe, but was not, in the event, really European. Not all the apparatus of Europe had been transported across the Atlantic, and this was often a gain; but not always. There was a deficiency in America which might be summed up as a contempt for the subtle and transcendent skills.

Japan, Russia, and America—these, together with the four great European states, made up the roster of genuine powers at the beginning of the century. Of the seven, five were entering a season of decline. One by one they were to be reduced by the first and second World Wars until, in 1945, a new Russia and a United States, torn from isolation and self-conscious in a newfound maturity, confronted one another over the ruins of the old empires. The two surviving powers at mid-century were marked not only by national styles of a piece with the past, but in Russia's case by two novel elements: the October Revolution, which had destroyed the incubus of archaic court structure, the imperial bureaucracy which had weighed down the nation's productive energies; and a philosophy of action, Marxism-Leninism, which was neither wholly old nor wholly new to Russia. For this state philosophy was itself remarkably consonant with the Russian past—a synthesis of the native populist tradition with that European rationalism and materialism which had always exerted a special fascination on the Russian mind—and it was informed by the old Russian passion for transcendent political theories. For how old a strain the messianic component is in Russian thought is attested by the host of medieval references in Orthodox chronicles to Moscow as "the third Rome," the "second Jerusalem," the "second Noah's Ark."

Thus for Russia and America, both given to purposive theories of history, there was something altogether fitting in this confrontation. To the Americans, who by 1945 had already been drawn into two wars in the confident expectation that evil in the world was a growth which might be extirpated root and branch, the Soviets were the ultimate challenge. It was not only the naïve who sensed an apocalyptic moment. "Surely," wrote George Kennan, "there was never a fairer test of national quality than this."

For the Soviets the moment seemed equally portentous. If the United States alone stood against them, then Soviet energy and the Marxist logic of history must bring America's collapse and pass sole leadership to Moscow. The results of this confrontation we have seen; the upshot was stalemate—containment, but mutual containment. Yet by 1950 events had begun to pull against this Soviet-American monopoly of politics: there was a new trend, an incipient trend at least, evident in the world. Where nations once had sought the protection and patronage of the two surviving great powers, or were compelled to accept them when the Cold War began, they now sought roles outside the static pattern of Soviet-American competition.

For history abhors categorical choices. The bipolar world

could not endure. The conditions which had produced it were already being rendered obsolete by events.

America had emerged from the second World War as a paramount, some might say *the* paramount, power because its productive apparatus was intact. Indeed, it emerged in 1945 vastly richer and more powerful than when it had entered the war four years earlier, having learned the trick of social mobilization on a titanic scale. Compared to this wartime mobilization, the preceding years of the New Deal were only a preliminary. The United States in 1945 was not, however, stronger in every respect: by the war's end there was something like an atrophy of the national will. This was partly a revulsion from the atomic attack on Japan; but more deeply it derived from the expenditure of *élan,* of emotion, of hatred even, necessary for the conduct of the war—we are not a nation which knows how to hate well or for very long. And it is no accident that each of our wars, for all their propaganda, has been succeeded by a time of revulsion, a retreat from commitment.

Russia, of course, had been devastated by war—more so than the majority of the states of Western Europe. But as a simpler society, less advanced and therefore less brittle, it survived with something of its spirit intact. There was another factor as well—the self-conscious role of the Communist Party, which subscribed to a theory of will. If Russia in 1945 was materially poorer than the United States, its large resources, coupled with this discipline, were enough to enable it to maneuver in postwar thrust and counterthrust. And it had ended the war on a note of national exultation; it suffered no guilt.

For these two surviving great powers the immediate postwar years were an experience both disquieting and intoxicating: they were alone in the world. The future was theirs to make—or destroy. Yet this sense of omnipotence was illusion; for Europe was not dead and could not be expected, either in its western or in its eastern halves, to remain forever in tutelage of America and Russia. And that self-conscious technology—

the rational manipulation of natural forces which is the unique product of the European mind—was stirring the great introspective and timeless civilizations of Asia. Thus the Soviet-American balance was due to be upset, not by a sudden shift of power to the one or the other, but by the modulation of the geopolitical terms in the world.

The beginnings of this reverse trend hardly date much before 1950. There was, of course, much talk in Europe soon after the war of a Third Force. This was a slogan, for it can hardly be called a movement, which appealed to curiously diverse Europeans: disillusioned intellectuals, crypto-Communists, irreconcilable Fascists mourning Hitler and Mussolini, ultraconservative industrialists and politicians who feared American economic hegemony—and the merely ordinary European who felt, amidst the ruins of derelict glories, a kind of shame.

The conditions for such a pluralism as these men and women called for lay in the future. The impulse behind the talk of the time was escapist: the Third Force sought to elude geography and history. And the Stalinists of that era aimed to encourage this pernicious sentimentality, for in the political and social vacuum of postwar Europe there could have been no real defense against the shock tactics of the West European Communist parties only recently and incompletely disarmed, reinforced by the threat of Soviet armies waiting beyond the Elbe. This was the era of the Stockholm Peace Appeal, of germ-warfare charges, of Ban-the-Bomb marches.

Soviet tactics in this era were, of course, not wholly offensive, but the kind of offensive-defensive suitable to a weaker side possessing certain important advantages—a superiority of will and a kind of political agility which is the consequence of the drill-master's approach to politics. One major aim of Stalinist strategy in those years was to obfuscate and disrupt, and so to prevent that Western attack on the East which the Stalinists, had the roles been reversed, would logically have mounted.

The Soviet efforts to dominate Europe failed. They could not succeed in the face of Marshall aid and an astute United States policy. As for the defensive component, there was, in fact, no real danger of Western attack, for all the emotive talk in this country of "liberation."

The lasting effect of this ideological battle over Europe's ruins was, so far as Western policy was concerned, to equate Third Forcism with a high-minded taste for suicide, at best, and with fifth-column activities at worst. In a bipolar world there was no room as yet for alternatives. But the same poverty of response which led the United States to transfer intact the technique of military alliance-*cum*-economic aid from Europe to the emergent states of Asia and the Middle East induced us to interpret later and fundamentally dissimilar neutralist movements as the old Third Force we had learned to dismiss—or fear.

The upshot of our own parataxis—this reading of one image for another—was to make us set ourselves against rising nationalist forces. Most significantly, it was to deprive us of allies—at least *de facto* allies. For in our fear of nationalist movements which refused formal alliance with us, we were resisting the political force that was the surest challenge to Russia's universal claims.

Yet a genuine Third Force was in fact developing: hardly had the lines of the bipolar world been drawn than there came the first shock. In 1948 Yugoslavia, a Communist state, a zealot Communist state, seceded from the Soviet bloc. The real issues were obscure in Yugoslavia for a long time, for the shared, or ostensibly shared, ideology of the contestants hid the outlines of what was a raw conflict of national wills. But that the rebuff to the Soviets was given by a Soviet state *in parvo* merely increased the seriousness of the affront, without in any sense altering the essential terms.

For the Kremlin, the Yugoslav breach ought to have come as a somber warning; it should then have been clear that there was a fatal strategic flaw in the Soviet effort to transmute the world into a unitary society whose center was Moscow.

How seriously these Soviets took themselves after World War II we can hardly recall today. The Soviet successes in incorporating whole societies seemed a demonstrable fact— with the exception, seldom noticed, that the Russians, both before and after the October Revolution, had won their chief successes against barely conscious societies—the Buryats, the Kazakhs, the Chechen-Ingush; or else against societies like the Ukrainians or the Turkmens, who, ignoring an ephemeral postrevolutionary year or two, had enjoyed no independent existence for centuries. As independent polities they had disappeared from view long before the rise of the modern state. Yet even in these weak and submerged states Soviet authorities who sought to temporize with nationalism by employing the fiction "Socialist in content, national in form" met surprisingly stubborn resistance.

Yugoslavia had been a modern or quasi-modern independent state—as indeed had been all the postwar satellites, willing or otherwise, in Eastern Europe. It was not that Marxism, or even Marxism in its Stalinist form, had failed to "take" in Yugoslavia in 1946-1948—quite the contrary. The revolution by which Tito imposed the Party's will on the country was a complex process, sharing elements of civil war, liberation movement, and a drive for social and national vengeance. While it did not express the will of a majority, it nevertheless was a formidable movement with native roots.

But the vigor, or popularity, of Communism in Yugoslavia was irrelevant to the issue. There would be Communist, conceivably Soviet, successes after the Yugoslav schism: China, the great prize, still waited. But it profited the Russians little if a weak inter-war Kingdom of Serbs, Croats and Slovenes was succeeded by a stringently unified state that subscribed to Soviet theories of economics and politics and yet rejected Soviet control. It should have been clear from mid-1948 forward that a dogmatic ideology, however vital and insistent, was in the twentieth century no antidote to nationalism.

Yet at the beginning, the Yugoslav experiment in schism was a precarious business. Success lay in the future; for a time the ideological issues obscured the fundamental lesson that a movement which pretended to universal validity and yet could not enforce itself on an adjacent and backward Slavic hinterland could hardly dream of enforcing its rule on the ancient and subtle civilizations of Europe and Asia.

In the beginning the dogmatic issues loomed large because the contestants, Soviet and Yugoslav, chose to invoke ideology to account for what was, at bottom, a political combat. The essence of the Cominform charge, if it was ever intended to be taken seriously, was that Yugoslav leaders were "opportunist" —that is to say, soft—and that the Yugoslav security police were insolent to Russians and Russian agents. There was much truth in the charge against the Yugoslav police, but none in the charge against the leaders. The Yugoslav economy was rapidly being transformed on the Soviet model. In Stalinist zeal in those days, the Yugoslavs far outdistanced neighboring loyal satellites like Romania, Bulgaria and Hungary.

The truth is that in this very zeal the Yugoslav leaders declared the size of their ambitions and the degree to which Soviet tutelage chafed them. It was only later that the Yugoslavs, in an effort to dignify their schism, produced ideological innovations, but these were, in the last analysis, a rationale after the fact. So far as ideology genuinely came to figure in this dispute at all, it centered on the issue of nationality—a "national road to Socialism" and even an implied and most un-Marxist conclusion that ultimate goals too might differ from state to state, from society to society. But the real Yugoslav innovations were practical; the country and its leaders had no real taste for disputation. What broke through the Marxist crust was a kind of local synthesis: an alien ideology not wholly irrelevant or uncongenial to the proclivities and needs of the country, a preference for administrative solutions somewhat less centralized than the Soviets preferred, and a freeing of the national taste for a kind of derivative Austrian *gemütlichkeit*.

But the details of the Yugoslav domestic compromise are not

really at issue here. The essential ingredient which distinguished the Yugoslav search for a position between the giant blocs was the element of *toughness* signally absent from the contemporary West-European Third-Force doctrines. It was a sign of the re-emergence of national will—an effective will—in a region brutally devastated by the war. It would be matched later on in Poland and Hungary. For here, for the first time, were defined the terms of the equation which was to confound both Soviet and Western policies in the succeeding decade: the ratio between the strength of the underlying native culture—its particularist sense—and the gravity of the imperialist provocation to it.

To formulate such an equation is merely to invoke a convenient fiction: social science, if there is a social science, cannot produce a parallelogram of forces. The states which later followed Yugoslavia's lead in asserting independence of the power blocs were essentially weak states. That is to say, they were nationalist, but in the beginning they had little effective power, military or otherwise; it was their good fortune to secede from the West, from a power system more benign than the Soviet.

They were also colonial states, largely of the Southern Hemisphere, "colored" states. One by one, they swung into neutralism—India, Indonesia, Burma, Egypt, Ceylon. The impulse behind the choice of neutrality was not, strictly speaking, the same as the Yugoslav—although they were later, in some degree, to join with the Yugoslavs and out of certain shared experiences and understood interests to fashion a kind of ideology of polycentrism. The issue of color, for one, was irrelevant in Yugoslavia. The Yugoslavs had a colonial past, as subjects of an imperialist Islamic power, Turkey, which lent a special fervor to their nationalism, but it was a colonial past different in kind.

Apart from this, Yugoslavia occupied a borderland of Europe, but its allegiance to European civilization was unquestionable.

Indeed, part of the Yugoslavs' impulse to free their country from the Soviet bloc was the conviction, deep if unspoken, that Yugoslavia, even in its eastern Orthodox districts, belonged to Europe in a degree that the Soviets did not.

The new Asian neutrals did not share this single-minded allegiance to European civilization. Their attitude was more complicated: if they envied Europe its technology and its organizational skills, that civilization had degraded them in the past.

The new neutralism in the Southern Hemisphere was, at least in part, a refusal by national leaders to commit themselves to what was in essence an alien quarrel. This is not to say that the Soviets, as a demi-European power, did not have significant advantages in appealing to the Asians. India and Russia, say, had had no dealings in the past; no memories of past wrongs marred their new-found friendship. Nor had the United States ever oppressed these regions. But the American attitude was more equivocal: we had entered into ties with European states that were Asia's former oppressors; too, our Calvinist predilection for simplified causes led us to hector and bully these new nations, equating their neutrality with a fondness for our enemies.

What the United States had yet to realize was that, by treating these newly enfranchised nations as *de facto* allies of the Soviets, we tended, at least for the short run, to make them so. This is a point which warrants some discussion.

There is a kind of tension in American political life between theories of personal freedom—tolerance for difference, eccentricity even—and an aggressive, conforming egalitarianism which functions by denying the possibility of difference at all. This is the egalitarianism which leads to that tyranny of the majority which Tocqueville recorded more than a century ago. Our wartime One World formulations were an extension of this denial of difference on an international scale. The need to see the world as a unitary phenomenon became fused with

our preference for quasi-ethical causes. The result was a kind
of obstinate national unreason which has sometimes been
associated with the name of a single Secretary of State but
which is, in fact, an American style.

As it applied to early postwar India, say, there was something
almost comic in this American style of diplomacy. For in the
Indian nation we met an opponent, though not a deadly opponent, even more given than we to an ethical view of history:
here was a clash of ethical formulae. There was, for example, an
Indian tendency to view the Soviet-American rivalry in an
unsatisfyingly equivocal fashion. The leaders of postwar India
were all British trained (indeed, one of them, V. K. Krishna
Menon, had been something of a Bloomsbury toff) but they
were still vastly influenced by a characteristically ambiguous
Hindu ethic. This is a religious view which abjures polarity—
that simple contest between Good and Evil which in the
United States assumes such clarity. It is the genius of Indian
religion to see evil incarnate in the good, an inseparable feature
of life. It was impossible for the Indians to conceive of the
postwar struggle in terms even remotely related to the American. What ensued was a dialogue of the deaf.

All this was painful at the time. But it is worth remembering
that this same Indian penchant for ambiguity was bound, in
the long run, to work against Soviet efforts to subvert the
country through the propagation of even more obstinately
simplistic political theories. In part it is this Indian abhorrence
of polarities, this plural view, which has gone far to make
democracy feasible there. India is one of the few places in the
non-European world where democratic theories of politics
show signs of taking root; and if this is so, it will have been
British models and the Hindu ethos which deserve the credit.

In other regions of South Asia somewhat similar forces
were at work, particularly in those states formerly under the
British raj. Neutralism in the Middle East—and by a kind of
extension in Moslem Indonesia—bore a somewhat different

stamp. Here there was no tradition of tolerance for ambiguities, no taste for ethical subtleties, indeed no predisposition to democratic solutions—for the genius of Islam (the very word means *submission*) is categorical. This was a region in an incandescent state at the end of World War II. The Moslem peoples had just thrown off, or were in process of throwing off, the grip of the European empires, at the same time as there had been established a new state, Israel, regarded by the Arabs as an intrusive European body in their renascent society.

The result was a virulent politics which inevitably challenged the tardy American interest in the Middle East. It was not, however, a promising region for Soviet operations either. The Naguibist *coup d'état* and the early phases of the Nasserite revolution in Egypt (and eventually, by extension, in other regions of the Arab world) coincided with an ideological phase in Russia hostile to all revolutions not under immediate Communist tutelage. By the time the Soviets had reversed their position, the revolution in the Arab lands was well under way, with characteristics to be discussed later.

Of the Indian and Arab forms of neutralism, one is quietest and reflective; the other is overcharged with emotion, *reactive* to any foreign intrusion. One is parliamentarian, the other authoritarian. Their inner genius is quite dissimilar, and it should be apparent that Soviet ideology—the issue of the Soviets as a white, demi-European power aside—cannot appeal equally to both. Still less can a single formulation, or even a subtle variation on a single theme—which is the best the Soviets can hope to produce in these varied regions—appeal to the host of newer states in Africa which have emerged in the last decade. These new nations of Asia and Africa are still more disparate. They have, in one degree or another, withdrawn from the Western bloc; but they have not thereby joined with the Soviets, or the Chinese. Indeed, it would be the gravest sort of error to treat them as a unity. The Yugoslavs and Nasserites have sometimes talked of a concerted diplomatic action, an organized Third Force, but the prospective parties have always tended to draw back.

The genuine significance of the neutral states has only come to be appreciated with the passage of time. There is still an overpowering tendency to treat neutralism as a *phase,* a way station on the road to incorporation into the Western system, defined as a "victory for democracy," or into the Soviet system. Incorporation into the Soviet system would be, to be sure, a catastrophe for American and European interests, and for the long-term interests of these states as well. But it is difficult to see what genuine affinity even the more authoritarian and statist neutrals have with Soviet theories of economics and society. This is the fallacy of the undistributed middle term. For if Soviet economic theories fall into the logical category "non-U.S."—as do Burmese economic theories—it does not follow that the Burmese and Soviet theories are identical, or even significantly related.

We would do better to understand that the philosophical possibilities of history are exhausted neither by Soviet nor American alternatives. The neutral area is not in fact a region for a contest between the Soviet and American world systems: it is a region emerging, or re-emerging, into history. In a century of the hypertrophy of nationalism their political and economic solutions will bear some resemblance to their cultural past— as did the Japanese synthesis a half century earlier. They will not turn capitalist, for as Tawney and Weber have noted, modern capitalism is closely related to the Protestant, or at least European, ethic. But these states will not, barring military conquest, turn Socialist either, in the Marxist or Fabian sense. These doctrines too are European and bear the stamp of a specific time and place. They may, however, opt for statist solutions, for many of these nations have an authoritarian past. But that is not the same thing.

By and large, both of the white superpowers are irrelevant to the concerns of these largely colored states: even in their earliest and weakest phase the new states have tended to behave as if they understood the distinction between themselves and the superpowers. Their independence of Eastern and Western blocs has been ratified by the passage of time. On a political plane, these states have created for themselves a role that in its effects on the Soviet-American competition resembles the part taken by Great Britain in the days of the European power balance. Their authority is largely negative: the ability to block Soviet and American initiatives. That authority depends on the precarious balance between the two major blocs, but it is no less power for that. They command at the moment no large economic or military resources, but their political influence extends throughout the backward Southern Hemisphere. In this respect the Third Force is more powerful than either the United States or the USSR.

In tracing the rise of pluralist forces in the world, we have thus far concerned ourselves with the neutral zone of Asia and Africa, states which have tended to view dispassionately the Soviet-American rivalry and to resist the giant powers' persistent efforts to incorporate them into one system or the other. The significance of these Afro-Asian neutrals has been to *deny* the pretensions of the superpowers, preserving themselves from involvement in the Cold War. Slowly this purely negative role has been superseded, in part, by the ability to undertake certain positive, if severely limited, initiatives in international affairs. The incorporation of Syria into an Egyptian union, forestalling Soviet plans, was such an initiative—within the confines of the Middle East, to be sure, on a local rather than a global scale. The exertion of a restraining influence on the Soviet government during the Congo crisis in the summer of 1960 was another. The effect these states have had on nuclear-weapons policy is a third. The power of these nonaligned states has been growing, within the United Nations and without. To a degree this rising influence reflects increasing political and economic strength. But the power blocs themselves have simultaneously become weaker, have tended to become more vulnerable to pressures exerted by third parties.

The Yugoslav case, we have seen, provided an early—almost premature—clue to the future of the great alliance systems. After the Yugoslav defection the Soviets won what appeared to be a brilliant success in China. Ostensibly they succeeded in detaching a former member, though under Kuomintang government a distracted and weak member, from the American alliance system and incorporating it into the Soviet world. As a nation of half a billion souls, this was an apparent accretion of power to the Soviets on a vast scale.

Subsequent events have tended to prove otherwise, for whatever the future impact of China on the world balance of power, it is already certain that this is no docile ally, still less a petty hanger-on, submissive to orders. *Mutatis mutandis,* the Chinese experiment has merely underscored the warning first administered by the Yugoslav schismatics. Yugoslavia demonstrated that mere allegiance to Soviet theories—to Socialism, as the Soviets like to put it—is no automatic gain for the Russian interest, except in the most sentimental terms.

In terms of classical *Realpolitik,* the Russian gains have proved singularly ephemeral. Even in the weak European dependencies Russia faces the colonialist dilemma: the old colonial powers of Europe found it impossible to exploit their dependencies without introducing the seeds of industrialism and progress, ideas which were bound to galvanize previously docile societies. Similarly the Soviets have introduced their Marxist leaven into the erstwhile feeble states of East-Central Europe. The long-range effect of their doctrines has been to stiffen societies which were once easy prey to the equally rapacious but economically less ambitious Nazis and even to an Austro-Hungarian empire which had raised bureaucratic inefficiency to something like a state dogma.

The Korean War marked the last point in time when the Soviets were able to mulct these client states; they did so at a cost to Eastern Europe, economic and social, which only became apparent after Stalin's death, when resurgent Polish and Hungarian critics for the first time spoke out with terrible bitterness. The ruinous effects of the intensification of already stringent economic plans in Eastern Europe—imposed as a direct consequence of the Soviet bloc's involvement in the Korean War—contributed heavily to the massive reaction against Soviet domination which transformed Eastern Europe in 1955 and 1956.

The self-assertiveness of the European satellites had begun to express itself after Stalin's death in 1953, though it is an open question whether the demonic policies being developed when he died might not in the long run have provoked an explosion bloodier than the one that came. After Stalin's death, throughout the years 1954-56, there was a quality of indecision, a loss of spirit, among the Communist parties of Eastern Europe which boded ill for Soviet ambitions. A slackness at the imperial center in Moscow was transformed into a kind of frightened insecurity in Warsaw, Budapest, and Prague. But contrary to containment's prediction, it was the *imperial* structure which had begun to prove weak—Soviet society itself had achieved an inner dynamic. The attention of Western politicians was, however, riveted on the essentially irrelevant quarrel for succession in the Kremlin so that the opportunities for political action in Eastern Europe during those years were allowed to slip by virtually unnoticed. But whatever the opportunities to exploit the cracks in the Soviet empire which were ignored by the Western alliance, it became abundantly clear from 1955 forward, particularly when Nikita Khrushchev sought a *détente* with the victorious Yugoslavs, that the Russians were about to acquiesce in a far-reaching revision of the terms of alliance in the Communist world.

The Soviets adopted the doctrine of separate roads to Socialism; this was a repudiation of their earlier unitary claims. The Russians were able to cling to the fig leaf of a unitary goal, however much the "roads" might differ; but no one ought to have been deceived. The consequences in Eastern Europe were

delayed for more than a year—but when they came they proved
to be revolt.

The issue in China was more subtle. The very size of the
country and the very brilliance of the Chinese revolution were
a challenge to the Soviets; apparently from the beginning
neither party to this delicate alliance needed to be told the differences of scale and quality which distinguished China from
the European satellites, though Stalin, a figure of genuine awe
even to Mao Tse-tung and Chou En-lai, found it possible to
hold the Chinese in check. With his death, the Chinese found
it expedient to speak out for heterodoxy; their intention almost
certainly was to weaken Soviet supremacy though they continued to be aware of the advantages of a loose Socialist alliance, a confederation, as it were, of like-minded states.

The impact of these Chinese tactics, which in the Soviet
orbit were always understood to spring from a deep national
sense, was unsettling. The Chinese continued to pursue their
own goals and to support the "separate roads" doctrine without
much understanding of the implications such a policy was
bound to have in states which had existed for centuries on the
borderlands of Europe and which considered themselves Western. The European satellites had been exposed to Renaissance,
Reformation, and Enlightenment, however diffuse these influences may have been.

The result was to unbalance a European alliance system
which the Soviets, even in the absence of Chinese meddling,
were finding increasingly difficult to control. There is some
evidence that the Chinese continued to support the Poles and
the Hungarians throughout the stormy months of the spring and
summer of 1956 preceding the great revolts. They did so, as
events would prove, not out of any taste for the liberalism
which characterized the revisionist critics of Soviet policy
in Eastern Europe, but out of an apparent decision to support
any movement, even remotely Socialist, whose effects would
be to cut down Soviet pretensions and central control.

In the event, they got more than they bargained for: Hungary and Poland threw out a series of challenges to Soviet authority—and Soviet theories of economics and society—which went far to undo the political gains won by the Russians in the aftermath of World War II. Yet if the alliance system was the loser, the Chinese, in the narrower national sense, were the gainers; for Soviet pretensions could not survive the 1956 revolutions wholly intact. It is no valid argument to maintain that the Soviets were able to put down the Hungarian revolt in blood. Apart from the fact that the Soviet experiment in frightfulness succeeded in damping the armed revolt itself, the Russians, who in conclave were forced to invoke Chinese ideological support in their effort to bolster their own shattered prestige, had lost status. The long-range effect of the 1956 revolts in Eastern Europe was as much to encourage the Chinese to self-assertion as anything else.

Nineteen fifty-six was a watershed of events—the end, if a single point in time can be chosen, of the postwar world. Suez and the revolutions in Hungary and Poland—in Poland a muted revolution, to be sure—dealt blows to the two alliance systems from which they have never recovered. After October 1956 nothing, East or West, could ever be the same.

Until Suez it might have appeared to a confident observer that the solvent of history was at work on the Soviet alliance only. The United States remained preoccupied with the Soviet capacity—by then much weakened, though few understood so— to subvert societies on the borders of the East bloc. But the solvent—and it had little or no connection with Soviet subversion—was at work on the West European alliance too, let alone the more gossamer alliance systems which the United States had woven in the Middle East and South Asia.

In Europe Marshall aid and native genius had done their work. Eleven years after the armistice ending the second World War there were few traces of ruin in Europe, few remaining psychic wounds. In France, England, Italy, Benelux

and the others there was an economic growth, a recovery of
élan which rendered Communist predictions obsolete, forcing
the Soviets, at the Twentieth Party Congress in 1956, to postulate a law of the "uneven development of capitalism" to ex-
plain Europe's renewal. In effect, they conceded the blasting
of their postwar hopes. Membership in the European Communist parties had fallen; a hard core of Party members remained, but their motives were as sentimental as they were
political. The Communists had lost their influence over the
populations at large.

There was prosperity in Europe, a sober prosperity. The
social malaise which had threatened to break out in revolution
on the continent and had even infected England was cured,
or much mitigated. There was an abundance of goods and
services surpassing prewar times. Postwar Europe, ruined
and defenseless, had once been certain only of Russian conquest: the doctrine expressed by European intellectuals in
those days was a verbalization of this sense of futility, the
absurd. By 1956 the prospect of such an attack came to be
dismissed. The United States found its European allies proving
more and more reluctant to contribute to the military alliance
and, as subsequent events would prove, to confide their secret
plans.

The underlying reality of the British and French attack on
Egypt was not that the military fiasco revealed an impotence
of our allies to act without us, but that it demonstrated their
dissatisfaction with our policies and their determination to
reassert independent roles for themselves. Suez was a defeat,
but it was not the paroxysm of dying empires: since 1956
France and Great Britain have grown stronger, not weaker.

With the return to power of Charles de Gaulle, a magisterial
man dominated by a sense of a *grandeur* in keeping with the
nation's past, France became capable of independent political
and military action—though de Gaulle soberly found it expedient to reduce French imperial commitments at the same
time as he reasserted the national dignity. The great break-

through for France was the achievement of a nuclear capability.

Britain too began again to launch diplomatic initiatives after Suez—and the United States, increasingly devoid of ideas and political energy, was compelled to follow. Indeed, in one shattering period, after the delivery of the first Soviet ultimatum on Berlin in the spring of 1958, it was the British and not the Americans who were able to summon the will to cope with the issue in any but the most frenzied terms; the British Prime Minister, until then a shadowy figure, went far in his fur cap, which he wore with a becoming *éclat*, to seize the imagination of an American public deprived of leadership, and of an American government almost eager to surrender responsibility.

The defeated Axis states, Germany and Japan, have remained in American tutelage, but their economic recoveries have been spectacular; they possess the material resources for independent roles. They hesitate over the implications: Japan has not yet quite recovered a sense of self-sufficiency; the Germans are hindered by the division of their country between East and West. But the disorders in Japan in the summer of 1960 were a warning; it would be rash to expect present power relations between the United States and Japan to endure much longer. And Germany's elections in 1961 will almost surely begin the end of its present status as political dependent of America.

Technology is altering the traditional foundations of economic and military power—from the classic iron and coal systems to new ones based in oil, electronics, and chemistry. More distantly we see the approach of an abundant nuclear energy which will have the effect of destroying the terms of economic geography as we have known them. Henry Kissinger has written:

In the era of what we now call conventional weapons, the force-in-being was not nearly so significant as the industrial potential and the mobilization base. ... Technology was relatively stable ... victory could generally be achieved only through a prolonged mobilization of resources *after* a war had started. . . . [Today] conditions have basically altered. Technology is volatile. . . . Every country lives with the nightmare that even if it puts forth its best efforts its survival may be jeopardized by a technological breakthrough on the part of its opponent. It knows that every invention opens up the prospect of many others.[1]

The revolution in weapons alone has already brought a quantum change in the relations between states. The age of nuclear plenty is now approaching. Its effects can be seen in the fact that Great Britain not only has its own nuclear arsenal but a powerful and skillful RAF strategic bomber force. France has its own atomic bomb, and must, in present terms, soon possess hydrogen weapons. Other states—Sweden and China are two obvious candidates—are certain to follow.

This means that the first period of the nuclear era—the era of polarization of strength—has drawn to a close, and the second, the period of the diffusion of power, is beginning. The consequences for the military balance in the world will be revolutionary. The long-range effects of nuclear-weapons technology is a topic we shall have to consider in detail below. For the present, it is enough to note that these weapons have the ultimate effect of making the small the equal of the great: there is no easily discernible ratio between size, productive capacity and wealth on the one hand and a nuclear destructive capacity on the other. The concept of "overkill" comes into play, for two, three, or ten times infinity is still infinity, as is one-half.

For the foreseeable future the diffusion of nuclear weapons is likely to go on. Even a nuclear disarmament agreement between the United States and Russia, which have an unspoken common interest in suspending the nuclear race, is improbable, if only because such an agreement is likely to prove unstable. Again Professor Kissinger has said:

No country can protect itself against *all* the technological possibilities increasingly open to its opponents. Conversely, an advantage once achieved will produce a powerful incentive to exploit it, for the scientific revolution which made it possible also ensures that it will be transitory.[2]

While the great powers might achieve the unprecedented diplomatic feat of an agreement to limit their own competition through inspection and controls, it is difficult to see that they could enforce a nuclear embargo on the world. We need extrapolate no more than a quarter century into the future to envision a time when the essential technology will be commonplace: it is highly unlikely, for example, that in such an era preliminary testing of nuclear weapons will be necessary at all. Nor in the light of the advance of technology are rocket delivery systems likely to remain an arcane study.

The Communist age that ended with Stalin's death, whatever its claims, was essentially a Russian age. While Stalin could not dispose of the material power wielded by Khrushchev, his word was unchallenged law in one-third of the earth; no man dared gainsay him, not Mao Tse-tung, not Chou En-lai, not Wladyslaw Gomulka. Nikita Khrushchev cannot make that claim. In absolute terms Russia's power is growing; in relative terms, shrinking.

While Russia remains a dangerous opponent, the blunt truth is that, for all its noisy threats, it has made no demonstrable inroads on the world in a decade. Such aggressive expansion as has occurred has, directly or indirectly, been Chinese—in Korea, Tibet, the Indian border regions, and Vietnam. And what has deterred Soviet expansion and blunted Chinese has been nationalism. Not the Baghdad Pact, not Soviet Communism, but Arab nationalism has dominated the Middle East; elsewhere, in Asia, Africa, the Caribbean even, the story has been essentially the same. And Communism's role, where it can claim to have damaged us, has been as eager second to nationalism. SEATO today is but a paper treaty, and the Baghdad Alliance is an historical fiction—rendered impotent, not by Soviet machinations, but by purely local events.

Nor has the Soviet Union escaped unscathed. There have been the Soviet failures in Syria, Iraq, the Congo—within the Communist empire itself. For against the force of nationalism the Soviet system has proved hardly sturdier than any other. The reality of contemporary Soviet power is the very reverse of that reality which confronted the world at the war's end. Material evidences of power the USSR possesses in plenty; but no longer can it radiate, in George Kennan's phrase, "the strange charm of its primitive political vitality." Nor even in the contemporary world are its quantitative victories, present or prospective, likely to prove enduring. We are entering an era of giganticism—in which giganticism itself has been robbed of all meaning. Under the arch of the nuclear deterrent the geopolitics of the world have been transformed.

PART TWO

The World Today

CHAPTER FOUR

Russia

> The Church of Old Rome fell because of its heresy; the gates
> of the Second Rome, Constantinople, have been hewn down by
> the axes of the infidel Turks; but the Church of Moscow, the
> Church of the New Rome, shines brighter than the Sun in the
> whole Universe.... Two Romes have fallen, but the Third
> stands fast; a fourth there cannot be.
>
> —*Theophilus of Pskov to the
> Grand Duke Basil of Moscow*

THE WORLD has been transformed, but our understanding lags
behind. It is as though we and the Soviets were armies awakening in the field to find the familiar contours gone from the maps,
the landscapes stripped and leveled. Moscow's primacy is
daily challenged by Peking, and the states of Eastern Europe
assert their individuality. The American alliance system is dis-
integrating before our eyes. New nations are rising in the world,
resisting our claims—ours and the Russians' alike—questioning
our purposes, seeking places of their own in the affairs of our
times.

This imposing rise of powers beyond the framework of the
Cold War and hostile to its threats and dangers has implications not yet grasped in either Moscow or Washington, nor—
more important—fully understood even in the capitals of Asia,
Latin America, and Western Europe.

Communism itself is changing. What it may become, especially in China, we do not know, though in Russia today the
movement, after forty years, seems more recognizably European
in form and for that more accessible to the outside world. In

both Russia and China, Communist society is sure to become more formidable in sheer material strength—in economics, technology, and military power. But it will not impose its style and ways on the variety of the world any more than the Protestant meliorism and progressivism of the United States is likely to seize the societies of Afghanistan and Senegal. Nor will the next few decades bring parliamentarianism to the tropic sweep of Asia and Africa or federalism to the world. Communism will unquestionably contend in the politically emergent areas, as will the example of Anglo-Saxon common law and French republicanism. But what will result will be beyond these institutions, and recognition of this fact is essential if we are to appraise the true character of the Soviet-American rivalry and the real nature of the test the Communist movement poses both to the United States and to the political development of the modern world.

The only prophecy possible is a negative one: the world will not conform to our parochial vision and ambition. Beyond that only trends and movements can be discerned, and for the shadowed glimpses they may afford of the coming decades it is worth looking closely at contemporary Russia and China and at the new nations—at their political and cultural roots and characteristics, the moods and needs that seem likely to influence their future.

The eight years since Stalin's death have transformed Russia —if not out of all recognition, still so profoundly as to confound those experts who claimed to understand this strange state best. Those supposedly immutable features of Soviet society —the "permanent purge," the supremacy of the police, the total prohibition of foreign contacts, the slave-labor camps, in short the absolute reliance on the stimulus of terror—all are gone or much mitigated. The next ten years will almost certainly accelerate this trend.

There has been a curious failure of vision, not only in America, but in the Western world as a whole, in dealing with the

Russians. It is not merely that we have failed to understand the inner dynamic of this aberrant society; we have failed to view it as a society at all. Partly this has been the result of that divorce from reality—the legacy of the war and the ideological policies of the thirties—which has distorted our Western view of the contest with the Russians. Not content merely with the categorical distinction between "our enemy," the Soviet government, and "our friends," the Russian people, we further abstracted reality and made it something like an article of faith that the Soviet government is not so much a government as an international conspiracy. We have believed that it is a conspiracy whose accidental locus is Moscow, but whose ambit is the world.

Some of our political men, and they have not always been excluded from the councils of serious policy, have been so engrossed in the exegesis of Leninist texts as to impute to the Communists a capacity to plan at a distance of half a century and to foresee the future in a detail remarkable for men supposedly blinded by erroneous doctrine. One might almost wonder if these Western analysts, like somewhat uncertain Scottish Presbyters, are not unnerved by the ambiguity of God's role in the universe—are not intimidated by the puissance of hell.

This extrapolitical interpretation of Russia has been a genuine defect of policy, not merely a sin of rhetoric; dogmatic aggression by the East has provoked a dogmatic reaction. The effort which the American government—and indeed the universities and foundations—has spent on elaborate Soviet researches has failed signally to produce useful insights into the nature of Soviet reality. If the Soviets have been guilty of viewing the Western world through the distorting prism of ideology, we have not done much better in understanding them. We have sometimes spoken of a Russian national interest—"the age-old dream of the Tsars," "Russia's historic drive for warmwater ports" are two usual formulations—but as a kind of casual afterthought, substituting for a serious analysis of what such a national factor might genuinely be in the mid-twentieth century.

Western thinking, reinforced by the horror usually felt for revolutionary movements by established states practicing a conservative economics, has strangely interacted with the Russians' own. For we have tended to view the Russian leaders as they believe themselves to be: as indeed the chiefs of an epochal movement, the vanguard of history—both more and less than human.

It is not that the more illusory Western theories are devoid of all substance: any dream touches on reality at some significant point. Indeed, the most pernicious point of contact is the Russian leaders' own view of themselves and their mission. It is their serious pretension that they are a new kind of man, motivated and acting in a new kind of way. But they are not. *Mutatis mutandis,* there have been like men and like states before, and there will be again. However, our political interpretations have acted to confirm the Soviet leaders in their conviction of uniqueness, with results which are hardly useful for the world's prospects.

The truth is that we have so deluded ourselves that we are not even certain of the effects of time on Soviet society: we are not, it would seem, altogether certain that they are subject to the laws of growth and decay. It was a Western conviction until 1956 that revolution in a Communist society was unthinkable: the omnipotent state would crush all possibility of dissidence. Orwell had compellingly argued that men in such a world could be robbed of the very vocabulary of dissent. A decade ago it was maintained that this society could never dispense with the most brutal and irrational features of Stalinism lest the state collapse overnight. But while Russia remains a tyranny, the unique institutions of terror—the secret police as a semi-independent state within the state, the terrible complex of forced labor camps, the purge as a mechanism of policy —have atrophied, to be replaced by something more subtle. We have so far forgotten what Stalinism was that we are not even able to measure the distance the Russians have traveled. Gradually they take on the look of a quasi-normal civilian state, rather than a police or military state.

Our memories are faded—a strange failure, when we consider how Russia commanded the attention of the world in the 1930's and 1940's. The press, the Sovietologists, invoke the epithet "Stalinist" without remembering, it seems, what it once meant. It is no service to truth to argue that Mr. Khrushchev, whatever his thick brutality, his willingness to throw troops against the Budapest rebels, is not qualitatively different from Stalin. We forget—it seems—Stalin's twenty million victims in Kolyma, Karaganda, and the other sub-Arctic death camps now closed. We forget the deportation of whole nations, the hounding and near-annihilation of small peoples like the Kazakhs and the Crimean Tartars, the insanity and terror of the *Yezhovschina;* the gangs of feral children, the corpses hauled off like cordwood during the state-induced famine of the 1930's; the "guilty" who stood before the courts and demanded their own blood as final act of expiation to the state, the ultimate lunacy of the Jewish Doctor's Plot on the eve of Stalin's death—half horror out of Kafka, half ideological pogrom.

We forget the very numbers: the Great Purge of 1936-38, claiming between seven and eight million victims, of whom more than half were murdered. A third of the membership of the Communist Party of the Soviet Union purged—some 800,000 persons alone, the dead including 6 out of 13 members of the Politburo, 1,109 out of 1,966 delegates to the 1934 Party Congress, more than a third of the elected deputies in the Supreme Soviet, nearly all the provincial Party secretaries, between 20,000 and 35,000 army officers, including 3 out of 5 marshals, 13 out of 15 Army commanders, 57 out of 85 Corps commanders and 110 out of 195 division commanders. We forget that an estimated 4 per cent of the entire populations of Byelorussia and the Caucasus were snatched away by this purge.[1]

If we were able to remember these things clearly enough

to contrast them with the Russian present, however distasteful to us that present may be, we could find a certain useful perspective. We would spare ourselves the near-fatuous invocation of the term "Stalinism" at every real, or fancied, international crisis. We would at least understand the term we use, and what it is that we mean to say.

None of this denies the continuing irrationality in Soviet ideology and policy, nor the obstinate ignorance with which the Soviets view history and politics. Pragmatism and a certain madness are bound together tightly in their ethos. But normality too is a powerful force. The demonic energy of the totalitarian state depends—as Hannah Arendt has observed—on the unfailing maintenance of the fictions by which it accounts for history. When this psychotic world is opened to the ordinary and the practical, the machinery of total control allowed to fall into disrepair, as has happened in Russia, there is ground for hope.

The task of Western diplomacy—indeed, the task of all the national diplomacies which confront this state—is to hedge it about, not in the hope of annihilating it, but in the hope of blunting its fantasies and allowing reality to break in. The task is to create situations in which madness is foiled and the forces of the ordinary and normal obtrude on the perfervid world of Soviet Communism. Our error so far has been to do this too little; Yugoslavia, Iraq, Hungary, Poland, have made a good beginning; if there is ever a serious rebuke to Soviet pretentions in China, it may well complete the work, convincing the Russians that there is no profit in carrying the light to such Gentiles.

We have done the opposite, accepting the Soviet claim to an abnormal, even transmundane power, grossly magnifying their capacity to intervene from Tokyo to Accra. The Soviet Union is a great power and a dangerous one. But theirs is an ideology not so much demonic as naïve; for it is their fixed illusion that history is a kind of simple calculation, that whatever its dialectical rhythm, it has led inevitably to them. They believe that revolutionary upheavals everywhere are some-how related to theirs—either a derivative, or at least a parallel, phenomenon, or a counterrevolutionary rejection. For Russia, the Soviets affirm, stands at a penultimate stage of history—she is the last stage but one, for "a fourth Rome there cannot be."

All this is no novelty to Russian political thought. Modern Russia, however, is something more than old Russia brought into the modern age. For modern Russia is a state sprung from ideological revolution, and it belongs to a definable historical category—the Ideologized State, the Messianic State—which seeks not merely to conquer the world but to alchemize it. The goals of such a state cannot be precisely defined. Its goals transcend reality and lie beyond time.

There have been other such states. The Moslem Caliphate of the seventh to tenth centuries was one; and, for dynastic Europe, revolutionary France was another. The phenomenon of *thrust* in these societies has been noted by Crane Brinton in his *Anatomy of Revolution:*

. . . Our revolutionists [in 1642, 1775, 1789, and 1917] all sought to spread the gospel of their revolution. What we now call "national-ism" is certainly present as an element in all these revolutionary gospels. But at least in the earlier years, and during the crisis of a revolution, crude notions of national expansion do not prevail. The lucky people to whom the gospel has been revealed wish to spread it properly abroad. In the messianic fervor of the crisis period, aggressive nationalism is not on the surface. This nationalism doubt-less helps drive the revolutionists on, and in the period of reaction it emerges into the light, barely if at all disguised as the "destiny" of a chosen people and its leader. The Jacobins announced that they were bringing the blessings of freedom to all the people of the earth, and such is the power of imagination that some people still think of Napoleon as agent of the new freedom. The Bolsheviks are still present to our generation as the great apostles of worldwide revolution. . . .

The Calvinists as Christians, of course, were ardent proselyters.

But the victorious English Independents were also capable of mixing their religious with political propaganda, were anxious to win the world. . . .

Perhaps the most important uniformity in our four revolutions is that as gospels, forms of religion, they are all universalist in aspiration and nationalist, exclusive, in ultimate fact.[2]

It is this factor of illimitable goals that makes Russia today such a difficult opponent. So far it has proved impossible to come to real terms with the Soviet leaders: like the crusader kings of Jerusalem and Antioch in an earlier age, they believe that an oath with the unbeliever is no oath at all.

It is futile to deal with the Ideologized State—so long as the first zeal lasts. But the capacity for ideological frenzy is not easy to sustain, the less so as that ideology is all-claiming in its pretensions. This is the fatal weakness of modern totalitarianism. A less demanding ideology, such as the older tyranny which made political claims but left its citizens unmolested in their private concerns, permits alternative satisfactions, a partial escape from rigors. The early Islamic state hardly attempted to regulate the area of the individual's obligation to family unit or clan. Nor did it attempt to organize productive activity or tap the economy for contributions to state or military power in any but the most rudimentary way. In the Arab borderlands of the seventh century the machinery for total mobilization could hardly have been conceived, still less operated—though in contemporary Byzantium or China, say, this was not entirely so. The result was an aggressive zeal which could last for more than three centuries. By contrast, there is no modern example of such a zeal lasting for more than a fifth the time. The outward thrust of the French Revolution was exhausted in less than twenty-five years.

Analogies to the Ummayad Caliphate, even Jacobin France, may seem farfetched; they are not. The capacity for ideological frenzy is not a modern monopoly. We ought not forget the quality of horror that the French Revolution engendered in the conservative societies of Europe and postrevolutionary America. With the France of the Directory, normal diplomatic inter-course was hardly possible. With the France of Napoleon—a kind of restoration of the norms of French life within the context of the revolution—such intercourse was barely tolerable, but only that.

There is a lesson, however qualified, in the history of these earlier movements. Aggressive ideologies, expressed in the Messianic State, are generally sprung from revolutionary movements, from a violent reversal of social and economic power relations *within* a single society or *between* that society itself and another subordinated to it. In the case of the French Revolution it was the rising commercial and industrial bourgoisie and their temporary proletarian allies who displaced the court and its administration. In Islam, it was the restive desert Arabs who changed roles with the Roman provincial bureaucracy of Syria and Egypt, and with the atrophied Sassanid Persian court at Ctesiphon.

The curious feature of these ideologized movements is that from the beginning there is a tension between universalist claims and the circumstances of their birth. For revolution, myth to the contrary, is seldom the sign of the decay of a society, but only of the decay of a ruling class. Nor is the decay of such an elite of itself enough to provoke revolution. For where the entire society is sunk in decay, revolution is hardly likely, but merely national and social extinction.

Revolution, then, is not so much a sign of exhaustion as the mark of vigor, of society in growth, though perhaps in un-balanced growth. And such aggressive revolutionary societies as the Arabs in the post-conquest eighth century, France in 1800, or Russia on the morrow of the October Revolution are likely to prove blatantly assertive in their narrow nationalist claims, however much, in the beginning, revolutionary zeal leads them to universal dogmas. The result is an inner contradiction which, as Brinton notes, grows with time: the messianic claims conflict more and more nakedly with the selfish demands

of the society itself. And the ultimate fate of the ideology—
which tends to be "bigger," more exalted, than the mundane
behavior of the state which gave the ideology birth—is to cut
loose from the ties of national interest and take on a life of
its own. And freed from the society of its origin, the ideology
tends to galvanize neighboring societies. These take over
elements associated with the revolution, but use these innovations for national purposes of their own.

Thus the wars of the French Revolution—which bankrupted
France and exhausted her manpower for a quarter of a century
—spread the doctrine of nationalism to Europe. And the result
was not French pan-European dominion, but guerrilla war
in Spain and, ultimately, the unification of Italy and Germany.
Where Valois and Bourbons had struggled for four centuries
to break the Hapsburg ring which threatened to strangle
France, the final result of the ideological impulse of the Jacobin
revolutionaries was to call into being, not an inefficient dynastic
union of Spanish and Austrian enemies, but modern Italy and
Germany—the states which in 1940 dismembered France.

For the desert Arabs the ultimate results of their movement
were no more satisfactory: within a century the purely Arab
Ummayad Caliphate was replaced by the Abbassids, expressing
the national interest of the non-Arab converts to Islam. The
ultimate beneficiaries of Islam were thus not the Arabs, who
quickly exhausted their expansive and creative impulse, but
the Persians, the Berbers, and finally the Turks, who held them
in subjugation for some four hundred years.

The nemesis of these revolutionary ideologies is their tendency to fragment, provoking a reaction against the state which
gave the alchemizing ideology birth. Has this already happened to the Soviets? The record of Yugoslavia, of China, and
of the satellite states of Eastern Europe is clear.

The breakup of the early Bolshevik ideology into national
ideologies is already well advanced. In Yugoslavia the Communist victory was hardly three years old before there was
schism. The development of national Communism in Poland

and Hungary was delayed another five years—when the death of Stalin and the weakening of imperial grip gave these countries their chance. The revolutionary upheavals in Eastern Europe in 1953-56 were both an ideologized reaction to Soviet dogmas by East German, Hungarian, and Polish converts to the creed, and a national rejection of that ideology. In the former cases, local Communists, more or less following the pattern of the Yugoslavs five years earlier, were seeking to convert Soviet ideology into a doctrine expressing national needs. In the latter aspect, the broadest elements of East German, Hungarian, and Polish societies were reacting to the alien element in Soviet ideology and attempting to reject it entire, or nearly so. But the distinction between the two impulses breaks down in practice; and in the East European revolutions themselves the two groups coalesced. On the Left there were significant groups who accepted Soviet theories in part, but wished to integrate these theories with local ethical, economic, or social norms—in short, to "revise" Soviet dogmas on national lines. On the Right the nationalist repudiation of foreign control did not necessarily extend to socialist economic theories. And in China the development of a variant ideology, expressing the national genius of the Chinese through dialectical innovations, had actually antedated the establishment of the Chinese Communist state itself.

Thus the effect of Soviet victories after the second World War—these victories were very largely a matter of picking up the pieces of shattered societies—has been to galvanize the states that surround Russia and to provoke national revivals which are, in the long run, unfavorable to the narrower Soviet interest. Soviet ideology and theories of the state and economy have converted the once passive regions of East-Central Europe and China into ultimate threats. For in 1917 the machine age, of which the October Revolution in Russia was an expression, had overleaped the fragmented states of the Danube and the Balkans, and had hardly reached the China of the Kuomintang. Today it is not difficult to envision a time when industrialism will have transformed these same regions. And Russia, which once bordered on a moribund Manchu dynasty or its unstable Kuomintang successor on the east, and the fragmented states of the Baltic-Danube-Aegean belt on the west, will be ringed in itself by industrially resurgent nations.

That the long-range effects of this geopolitical transformation of the Russian borderlands can be favorable to Russian national interests is hardly likely. There is no need to predict war, or even a physical struggle at all, between Russia and China, or Russia and its European satellites, to perceive the disadvantages to the *Russian* interest of this trend—whatever vindication of ideology the Soviets may see in the spread of Marxist-Leninist doctrine.

For these reasons, Eastern Europe remains an uneasy zone of Russian imperialism—and China does not qualify at all. We cannot expect a *uniform* rejection of Soviet ideology, or even of Soviet presence itself in all these disparate regions. Even the European satellites are anything but uniform: Poland, Hungary, and the western regions of Czechoslovakia have old ties to Western Europe. But Romania and Bulgaria are something else again; they belong to that Orthodox world that engendered Russia, as a glance at their traditional art and architecture will demonstrate. That there was a narrow prewar French- or German-speaking elite in these countries is not the same thing as a long-term involvement in the history of the West.

Thus it is difficult to see the Russian occupation or presence as an affront to Bulgaria equal to the affront given Hungarian or Polish sensibilities—and, in the event, we have seen none. The anti-Soviet revolutions, quite predictably, have come in the aggressively Catholic, aggressively anti-Russian satellites, Hungary and Poland, or in East Germany—all of them states tied to the Western world. In Czechoslovakia the reaction to Soviet imperialism has been weak; but by the standards of its neighbors, Czech nationalism has been weak: there is a long history here of accommodation to national degradation, though it is a history for which the Western world shares blame.

Yet even the most passive regions of East-Central Europe are more westernized than Russia: what they have *sought* is more Western, if not what they have done. Conceivably even in Bulgaria and Romania the ultimate effect of this difference will be to dissolve the alliance, if external factors prove favorable. There is even no certainty for Russia that the last word has been heard from the nationalities within its own borders. The Soviet Union holds the territories of a dozen submerged states; the political unity we know and speak of as permanent is the accomplishment of less than a century.

Russia today stands on the threshold of plenty: it is very close to becoming a have-state, at least as one-half or one-third of mankind defines the term. In a sense Russian evangelism, its preoccupation with saving the world—and stopping time—has been a kind of compensatory formation, a consolation for material deprivation. Messianic politics can weaken amidst abundance; but we must not overestimate this factor, for the twentieth century has taught us the meaning of the irrational in man. It is a naïve Fabianism to expect that mere economic abundance will of itself counter the dark flaw in man, turning a psychopathic society to peaceful growth. But it is safe to say that Russia today is a society only half-mad: it gives evidence of none of the transcendent madness of Nazi Germany, nor even of the unalloyed Orwellian horror of the Stalinist thirties. For Communism, whatever its defects, does not, like Nazism, spring from a satanic repudiation of the rational element in man. It is a perversion of the rationalist impulse—but a perversion only. As this society is held in check, as its messianism is rebuffed, as the risk of loss through foreign adventure is borne in, there is ground for hope that the force of reason may begin to prevail.

For more and more the Soviet political drive for the world takes on a traditional look; the Russians are inclined to seek less the *fata morgana* of universal empire than an influence and a respect in world affairs which, they conceive, is in keeping with industrial and technological success. It is difficult to believe that the ordinary Russian is any longer much concerned for the ideological well-being of Afro-Asia or Latin America—except in the vague sense that Americans assert that the world some day must share the American dream. The progress of proletarian revolution—the inevitable progress, is the usual formulation—has become increasingly an empty slogan, to be repeated at May Day festivals.

All this is ultimately the effect of Stalin's innovation—the doctrine of Socialism in One Country. For it is true that in the early years of the revolution the national element hardly figured; it was the universal messianic dream that counted for most. And Lenin had looked West. A Herodian intellectual, he had turned his back on much of the Russian past of obscurantism and crime; he, self-conscious heir of the Enlightenment, deplored it. He had looked West for support in 1917, believing that if proletarian revolution were not to break out in Germany, France, England—in the advanced nations of the West—the October Revolution, that sport of history, must fail. "Our backwardness has thrust us forward," he said in April 1918, "and we shall perish if we are unable to hold out until we meet with the mighty support of other countries." [3] But the world's refusal to conform to doctrinaire expectations threw Russia back on her own not inconsiderable resources. The result was the Russianization of the ideology: in this second phase, coinciding more or less with Stalin's lifetime, the Communist movement became a Russian movement.

It is only now, long after the *Vozhd's* death, that we see the morning of a third phase—the fragmentation of that pan-Russian and imperial dream.

CHAPTER FIVE

China

> [A nation at peace breeds] the Six Maggots, to wit, Rites
> and Music ... ; the cultivation of goodness, filial piety, and
> respect for elders; sincerity and truth; purity and integrity;
> kindness and morality; detraction of warfare and shame at tak-
> ing part in it....
> Concentrate the people upon warfare, and they will be brave;
> let them care about other things, and they will be cowardly....
> A people that looks to warfare as a ravening wolf looks at a
> piece of meat is a people that can be used.
>
> —*Shang Tzu* (d. 338 B.C.)

IT IS MORE than a decade now since the south China campaigns
—they do not merit the name of battles—which ended with
the expulsion of Chiang Kai-shek and the Kuomintang government from the mainland of Asia. The years since the establishment of the Chinese People's Republic have merely underscored the lesson of that titanic civil war: it was not Russia
that won it, nor America that lost it. It was, for all the boasts of
the Russians and the angry rhetoric in Washington, essentially
a Chinese internal affair, though vaster interests could not but
be affected by an event involving 600 million souls, nearly one-
fifth of mankind. It may well be in the long run that it was the
Russian national interest that was more seriously injured by
Mao's victory than ours. It is difficult to see that the substitution
on Russia's eastern flank of a cohesive and self-assertive power
in place of a congeries of distracted and enfeebled provinces
can have been a proper aim of Soviet policy, except as conceived in terms of the most naïve ideological preoccupation. For

Russia today incorporates important provinces of the outer Chinese Empire, as that Empire flourished in the days of the Han, the T'ang, and the early Ch'ing; the borders of Russia and China march for thousands of miles. By contrast America and China are a quarter of the globe apart.

As the distinction between China and Russia's European satellites has become clearer, we see the Chinese civil war as a victory for Communism with a difference. In important ways that war conformed to the grand movement of Chinese history, that cyclical process of dynastic growth and decay so much at variance with the histories of the West. Foreigners, Russian and American, for all their good or bad intentions, could not change the course of the struggle; its magnitude dwarfed even the capacity of the super-powers to intervene. The Russians were far from understanding where the balance of revolutionary probabilities lay. They were skeptical of Mao's prospects, or affected to be so, for there are ambiguities in Russia's wartime and early postwar China policies which the government in Peking is unlikely to have forgotten.

The main direction of Russian action at the close of the Japanese war was to demand short-range concessions which, by outraging Chinese sensitivities on the issue of extraterritoriality, might have been expected to compromise the Communists' reputation and their prospects of victory. Stalin had recognized Chiang Kai-shek as the head of the Chinese government throughout the war and for several years thereafter, though it is true that he treated the Kuomintang government with a studied contempt. By demanding concessions which restored Imperial Russian holdings lost to the Japanese in 1905, he was, in effect, reconstructing the situation which existed in the aftermath of the Boxer Rebellion. And as if that were not sufficient affront to the Chinese, Manchurian industry was dismantled and shipped to the Soviet Union as a "reparation" against defeated Japan without reference to legitimate Chinese rights or needs.

It is unlikely the Soviets foresaw an early Communist victory in China. By contrast the Americans, who accorded the Chinese the wartime courtesy of labeling them a great power—indeed making them a charter member of the Big Four—and extended to them the sum of $1,564,698,000 in economic and military aid, could not in any real sense stiffen a government which was already rotten within.*

But the legacy of that civil war, in which America's champion was so disastrously beaten, and of the later American military collision with the Chinese in Korea, has been a special bitterness in Sino-American relations. Nearly a decade after the Korean armistice it is still virtually impossible for Americans to discuss the China issue in a climate of dispassion. The Sino-American war of 1950-53 ended technically in a stalemate, but it was, in the larger scheme, a defeat—an especially bitter defeat in that once Korea's 38th parallel had been crossed there was no alternative to defeat that would not have been still crueler. As Raymond Aron has said:

If the Americans, after having landed at Inchon and destroyed the North Korean army, had voluntarily halted at the old demarcation line they would have been able to claim that they were the victors and been acknowledged as such. . . . But they had pushed on to the Yalu in order to re-establish the unity of Korea by force. They had failed. Certainly . . . the Chinese in their turn had failed when they attempted to fling the Eighth Army into the sea. . . . But the United States is the strongest power in the world. Morally, America's non-victory was a defeat, as the Chinese non-defeat was a victory.[2]

The irony of this passage of arms was that the Americans, historically the champions of China's liberties and the guarantor

---

* It is difficult to see, for example, how more generous United States military aid could have been useful to Chiang when a prize like Mukden could surrender to the Communists after the briefest of skirmishes. The superiority of the Communist armies (whose best equipment was largely captured Japanese matériel, markedly inferior to Chiang's American arms) was increasingly a moral superiority over the Kuomintang; peasant and intellectual alike treated the Kuomintang as an irrelevance. By January 1949 the Kuomintang commanders of Peking and Tientsin handed over their charges without a fight. As one observer, Hugh Seton-Watson, no friend of the Communist cause, has put it, "The last stages of the Communist advance were a triumphal parade." [1]

of her independence against the imperialist powers, were the ones who gave the Chinese their first taste of victory against a white power in something like two centuries. It was the Chinese success in Korea, not the sham battles of the civil war, which established Peking's military reputation. It ratified the Communists in their control of the mainland. Until the Korean armistice, it might be said, the issue remained in some doubt.

The later effect of the American failure was the gradual waning of our influence in East Asia. Our hold today is precarious; conversely, Chinese prestige and power—the two are not necessarily synonymous—have grown enormously in the past ten years.

Indeed, China has emerged as the great riddle of contemporary history: compared to the Chinese, the Soviets today are an open society, and the fascination which the Russia of the 1930's and the 1940's exerted on the world is now the special possession of Peking. The dread experienced by the outside world is compounded by distance and mystery—and by a quality of the irrational as well. It is difficult to avoid the impression that part of the Western horror of the Chinese spectacle lies in its racist implications—the Yellow Peril fused with the Red—and there is a fear, born of guilt, which is a projection of our own troubled consciences. We know in some sense we have reaped the whirlwind in China. The aggressions of Peking —against the Koreans, the Tibetans, the Mongols, indeed the internal aggressions against the Han peoples themselves—may be a moral outrage. But they are a kind of retribution of history.

"Let China sleep," said Napoleon. "When she wakes, the world will be sorry." But we have wakened her—we, the Russians, the Japanese, the British, and the rest. For more than two centuries the Western world inflicted a series of calculated humiliations on this ancient, isolated, and profoundly original civilization, treating the serene Middle Kingdom as a kind of fantastical and enfeebled giant whose diplomatic pretensions and court decorum were themselves a legitimate cause for a resort to war. The nineteenth and early twentieth centuries were the winter of Chinese degradation; the Manchu power which had checked the Russians at Nerchinsk fell into decay. The efforts of this wretched dynasty to preserve the integrity of the empire merely provoked new Western aggressions against the national self-esteem: China in 1900 managed to avoid the fate of India and never quite fell under colonial subjugation, but this must have seemed to a patriotic Chinese like a distinction without a difference. China's traditions were mocked, her wealth appropriated, her ports forcibly opened to the opium trade; she was seldom the object of disinterested pity, except perhaps in the United States, and not really even there. At the time of the Boxer Rebellion, that lunatic Chinese effort to throw off foreign oppression, the German Kaiser was able to exhort his troops to show no mercy on the Chinese, to retaliate for the murder of the German ambassador "like Huns."

To confront the post-industrial age into which she has been wakened, China has seized on the worst of her past—the traditions of centralized autocracy, burcaucratic oppression, alliance between ideology and the state—and fused it with a terrible corruption of the Western Faustian dream. We have deluded ourselves for years with the image of filial China, antimilitarist China, the China of Confucius, Chuang-tzu, and the Sung painters' inner eye. There is another China which, in America at least, we have found it convenient to ignore. There is the China of the military dynasties—the Han, the T'ang, the early Ch'ing—the China of Ch'in Shih-huang-ti, the First Universal Emperor,* who willed that the whole world be walled off

---

* The political career and theories of Shih-huang-ti would repay study. "By mass exchanges of population he succeeded in breaking down the most stubborn regionalism. . . . He divided the empire into thirty-six commanderies, each directly administered by a civil governor, a military governor, and a superintendent. His minister Li Ssu standardized the written [language] throughout the empire. . . . Furthermore, 'he standardized laws and regulations, weights and measures . . . even carriage axles.'

"At the instigation of his minister Li Ssu, this Chinese Caesar in 213 B.C. ordered the destruction of the classics . . . a measure which has earned him the hatred of the literati throughout the ages. . . . In the most divided and most

and saw it done. There is the China of Pan Ch'ao, who ravaged the oases of Central Asia and ground their pleasure palaces to dust.

The truth is that American political theories, wedded as they are to a belief in the supremacy of the rational factor, can hardly begin to cope with the Chinese tragedy. Against the backdrop of this grave spectacle it is hardly noteworthy that America as a nation is unjustly made the victim of Chinese xenophobia, that abiding hatred of the foreign devils, the *Yang kuei-tzu*. China, an ancient and complex civilization profoundly alien to our own, is swept along in a dual movement of history: for the past half century we have been witnessing the chaos and terror that in China traditionally attend the collapse of a ruling dynasty. And this cyclical movement of Chinese history is compounded, and dreadfully compounded, by the radiation of the Industrial Revolution into the non-European world.

There is a rhythm to Chinese history which is its own; there is no easily discernible progression of phases—"ancient," "medieval," "modern"—as distinguishes the histories of the Western world, or even the Near East. This history is a dynastic history—a series of beads strung on a thread: native Chinese political theory has generalized from the phenomenon, and interacted

---

feudal of countries, his caesarism was able in some twenty years to create a centralization strong enough to last twenty-one centuries. In short, he was one of the mightiest geniuses to whose lot the reshaping of humanity has fallen." [3]

It is worth adding only that the empire founded by Shih-huang-ti—a man who totally annihilated his enemies and affected the sensibility of China for more than two thousand years—collapsed within four years of his death. The Ch'in dynasty fell in a welter of civil war; the beneficiary of Huang-ti's innovations was the dynasty of Han—founded by an upstart penniless adventurer, Liu Pang, the son of a peasant, who emerged from the ensuing bout of anarchy and murder.

This distinction between introducing innovations which permanently affect the economic and social order of a nation and being able to found a dynasty, or political movement, which will itself endure is worth bearing in mind when considering the likely course of events in China over the next half century. History is full of examples of men or movements which have pulverized a society for the ultimate benefit of others. This is, in Arnold Toynbee's image, to play Caesar to Augustus, Hercules to Jove.

with it, so that theory reinforces fact. In this theory "the power of every dynasty springs from a Virtue (*Tö*) ... which passes through a time of fullness, then declines and after an ephemeral resurrection, becomes exhausted and is extinguished. The dynasty *ought* then to be extinguished, suppressed, for *it no longer has heaven on its side.*... [The] heavenly mandate is always temporary. Heaven is changeable and inexorable.... Every dynasty which retains power when its time has passed ... is a usurper. The founders of the [new] dynasty whose hour has come, fulfill a heavenly mission by suppressing the dynasty that has become out-of-date and maleficent. They are the ministers of divine chastisement, and their victory is [itself] the proof that heaven has entrusted to them its mandate (*ming*)." [4]

Even a cursory reading of Chinese history will confirm the principle: one might add that events at the end of the Kuomintang "dynasty" confirm it as well. Chinese history is replete with ephemeral dynasties which spring up in the wreckage of the old, only to be cut down. In this sense the Communist government at Peking is only the latest in a series of dynastic regimes to establish itself in China; it has done so according to the familiar pattern of secession from the central authority and mounting an insurrectionary war. Nor is the proletarian origin of the Communist movement's leaders or their social reforming zeal a valid distinction. China is not by tradition a society without mobility; its dynastic founders have as often as not been humble men, peasants, enlisted soldiers, bandits even; and the reforming zeal is an old element in China.

Yet if the Communist government is understood as a dynastic government in a context of Chinese history, it is a dynasty with a difference. It is a dynasty which simultaneously expresses the native Chinese reaction to the encroachments of the Western world and seizes on the technology and political techniques of Europe to reinforce its power. In this sense, it is self-conscious, "scientific," to a degree unknown in the Chinese past, though the career of a reforming emperor like Huang-ti provides a precedent for stringent Communist actions. There is at least one earlier movement in nineteenth-century Chinese history which provides a still closer analogy—the T'ai P'ing, or Great Peace Rebellion. For this was, like Chinese Communism, a syncretist political movement which sought to amalgamate the lessons of the Western world, so far as they could be understood, to a Chinese nationalism and social ideal. The difference in the case of the T'ai P'ings, led by the son of a poor farmer, who received instruction from a Protestant missionary near Canton, was that they sought to assimilate to an earlier wave of westernizing influence, Christianity, rather than the secularized Western religion, Marxism, which entered China in the twentieth century. Kenneth Scott Latourette has written:

> To the [T'ai P'ing] movement [1850-64] were attracted a number of dissatisfied elements, and it was, in part, an agrarian revolt, one of a long succession in China's history. It differed from the others in its religious content, derived from Christianity and therefore from the West. It destroyed idols, it utilized a Protestant translation of the Bible, it had baptism and forms of worship which were in part adaptations from Christian sources and it observed one day in seven for worship. It . . . was sternly against the use of opium, alcohol, and tobacco. . . . Yet it . . . did not teach the cardinal Christian ethical principle, love, [though] it advocated social and economic reform, including the redistribution of the land. . . . It was intensely Chinese and insisted that foreigners acknowledge the supremacy of Hung Hsiu-ch'üan as Emperor and religious leader, for it claimed universality for its faith. The T'ai P'ing movement gained temporary but destructive success. . . . Owing to the weakness of the Manchu regime, and in part to their zeal and organization, the T'ai P'ing forces won considerable initial victories. . . . Hundreds of thousands perished. Much of the Yangtze delta was laid waste, and some of the best libraries were burned.[5]

The claim of the T'ai P'ing faith to universality is another example of a messianic movement sprung from revolution which we have had occasion to examine in the context of Russian history: the aim of the T'ai P'ings was an Ideologized

State. The nativist element in this mid-nineteenth-century movement is attested by the name T'ai P'ing itself, borrowed from another peasant revolutionary movement some fifteen centuries earlier which overthrew the dynasty of Han.

China then is the second of the non-white states of Asia to adapt to the technological revolution, that movement of world history which began in the British Isles two centuries ago. Like Japan, which preceded her into the industrial age by seventy-five years or more, China reacted to the challenge of industrialism and ideology in the style of her past. But unlike Japan —essentially a pluralist society which encompassed the rival claims of family, clan, feudal lord, religious order, Shogun, Emperor, and individual, and in this sense approximated to the Western societal ideal—China was, and is, a "hydraulic" society (in Karl Wittfogel's expressive term), monolithic, ponderous, and unitary. It assimilates to a recognizable type of Oriental despotism: its ethos is profoundly hostile to individualist theories of personality and the state. China reacts to the present in her traditional style, while partaking also of that measure of political and social hysteria which is the mark of the other new states of Asia and Africa emerging into the industrial age.

All this should be sufficient to demonstrate the futility of viewing China in a foreshortened perspective, as if the meaning of her actions—and future—were to be determined by the categories of modern politics alone. The social paroxysm of contemporary China dwarfs our political conceptions; if there is any consolation in this awesome spectacle, it is that this is a national movement—a national Communism—of a peculiarly ugly sort. China's Asian neighbors are unlikely to wish to emulate this tragedy, however rapidly the Chinese nation, marching in lockstep, may drive steel production upward. The newly emergent African nations, dazzled by the specious analogies between the semicolonial Chinese past and their own, may for a time fall under her spell. But it is difficult, in view of the simple geography and logistics of the situation, to see how

such a political influence could be converted into a power to
direct the activities of those states, or into action directly harmful to the real interests of the Western world.

Certainly it will prove impossible to maintain the cordon
around China; the new states will open diplomatic relations, if
only to frighten and intimidate the West. But even as a political influence the prestige of China can be overemphasized.
The recurrent fears which seize the West—Chinese intervention
in Algeria, in the Congo, in Cuba even—have some of the
quality of psychopathology. The danger in Africa surely is less
a Chinese hegemony, or even an emulation of China, than a
reversion to tribalism or some new horror, pan-racialist perhaps
in its appeal to Negro Africa, but unlikely to include the quite
racially and culturally distant Chinese. Here our own latent
racism afflicts us—the category "non-white" which blocks out significant distinctions is meaningful to white men only. Within
this gross racist oversimplification, which victimizes the most
assiduously liberal thinkers of the Western world, there exist
differences abysmally clear to Bantu, Hindu, Berber, and Han.
It is not so much, it would appear, that China has seized the
imagination of the "colored" nations as that she has seized the
imagination of America.

One by one Communist China's neighbors, the Burmese, the
Thais, the Indonesians, the Indians, have turned against her.
If the Japanese still keep their illusions about Chinese intentions, it is largely because we Americans have kept them too
long in postwar political tutelage, shielding them from responsibility. It is the military and not the ideological containment of China which is likely to prove the most vexing problem
of the next decade. China espouses an arrogantly challenging
theory of war. Yet it is just possible that we and the Russians
will find a tacit common interest in checking the Chinese.

It is said that economic interests bind Russia and China, as
does devotion to a common revolutionary ideal. This is debat-
able. They are an ill-matched pair: their phases of revolutionary development are dissimilar; one is land-rich (indeed

holds lands formerly Chinese), the other is land-poor; one enjoys a favorable ratio between natural resources and population, the other stands at the brink of Malthusian tragedy. Most important of all, the geography of history has placed the Soviets adjacent to a stabilized front in Europe, to a Middle East in the flood tide of national revival: there are no easy conquests for the Russians. By contrast, in Asia the situation that tempts the Chinese is still fluid—China, in a stage of early industrial maturity, is tempted to exploit her relative industrial and military advantages over the weak states on her borders still mired in the stage of pre-industrialism.

In Russia the Communist ideology is invoked essentially as a kind of amalgam of society, a stimulus to industrial and social *élan,* but practical interests militate against expansionist adventures. In China the terms of the ideology still coincide with the temptations of *Realpolitik;* the two are one. Thus to speak of an ideology binding Russia and China is to place a faith in that ideology which the events in Yugoslavia, in Hungary, and in Poland do not commend. Nor, if tensions between Russia and China are further exacerbated in the next ten years, can we expect economic interest alone to hold the Chinese: it did not hold Tito.

Yet even China's Asian frontiers are not so easily crossed as all that. She can, of course, launch a simple assault on Asia, and if this is prevented it will not be the fiction of SEATO which does it. The United States will go to war for neutral India as resolutely—or reluctantly—as for its client Thailand. The Chinese know this, and they must know as well that their neighbors will resist them, as Tibet has fought, and by so doing increase the danger of a general war in which it is entirely possible the Russians would be reluctant to join. For if Europeans ask whether the Americans will risk Chicago for London or Paris, is it so certain that the Russians would risk Leningrad for Canton or Peking?

For China to launch aggressions beyond the area of its historic claims—the regions it controlled before the breakup

of Manchu power—would risk a nuclear holocaust. The Chinese
may affect to believe that war will leave them, relatively speaking, unscathed, since as a rudimentary society numbering 600
million they would survive essentially intact. They are unlikely
genuinely to believe this—especially if their Soviet allies have
done the work of military education. Their celebrated ideological quarrels with the Soviets center on the issue of war—or
ostensibly they do. But there is another factor at work: the
Soviets have consolidated their society; the Chinese have not.
Talk of peace—of "peaceful coexistence"—is as much a solvent
of national discipline in the Communist world as in the West
and in neutral Asia. The Khrushchevian doctrines inevitably
breed "the Six Maggots"—while, as the Realist philosophers
once formulated the doctrine, "a people that looks to warfare
. . . is a people that can be used."

But in any case, the loudly advertised and strident belief in
the efficacy of war, if it is a belief, is fatuous. The loss of 300
million persons—the magical 50 per-cent figure so often cited by
the Peking ideologues—would leave the Chinese nation pros-
trate, their nascent industries in ruin, disease and famine ram-
pant, the prestige and power of the central government which
had invited this catastrophe and found itself powerless to miti-
gate it equally in ruin. Indeed, one is tempted to say that the
only possible beneficiary of such a lunatic Chinese aggression
would be that force which has traditionally benefited from the
collapse of central authority in China—the nomad power. For
there has been in Chinese history a rhythmic interaction between the Desert and the Sown, the peasant and the nomad
herder. In periods of effective central authority the peasant has
intruded on the steppe; in times of disaster the nomad hordes—
Kitan, Ju-chen, Mongol, and the rest—have turned the peasant fields to grass. If this seems a farfetched prospect—re-
crudescence of central Asian nomadism in a post-modern age
under conditions of collapse of authority—we ought to consider
the likelihood to our Victorian forebears of a Western world
in terror of Peking.

In the immediate arena of political action the obvious course open to the Chinese is the whole range of subversive and irregular military operations beyond their borders. But here the rising tide of nationalism blocks them. As Mao Tse-tung has acknowledged, an irregular campaign is futile without political support in the war zone, and the events of the past thirteen years have supported this notable theorist of guerrilla war. "We are the fish, and the peasants are the sea," he is quoted as once saying; but where nationalism has found expression in regular governments, governments not compromised by a too close identification with the Western interest (for this is perceived as colonialism in disguise), the Communists have failed. We Americans have tended to identify each disorderly movement in China's border regions with Communist subversion. In Indochina, as earlier in Greece, it is true that military support from abroad was a necessary condition of sustained guerrilla war; but again, as in Greece, it would be an error to suppose that the mere fact of foreign support for the guerrillas told the whole story. There was a native issue as well—in one case an antipathy to a continued French colonial presence, in Greece to a rightist government which had forfeited the support of major segments of the Greek population.

The Chinese are mounting a sustained effort to subvert the liberties of their neighbors; but propaganda is a much overestimated weapon of modern war, or quasi-war. It functions best when a genuine issue exists to exploit; but seldom are such issues available to foreign powers. The Chinese themselves as a race are unpopular in southeast Asia—and for the Chinese seriously to consider that they can profit from lighting the fires of anti-Americanism in Malaya or Indonesia is rather like those in the West who believe they can unhinge the Soviet Union by invoking the very real issue of anti-Russianism among the Ukrainians.

The Chinese reputation in Asia stood highest when in fact the Chinese behaved most convincingly—as if they meant the things they said about nonintervention and coexistence; for they were good things that they said. But Tibet, the nationality disputes in Indonesia, and the Sino-Indian border disputes have changed all that. The Chinese cannot have Tibet and *Panch Sheel* too.

There are likely to be no certainties in dealing with China for a good many decades to come. The Chinese giant is in a perfervid state. The best hope of a military check on China, however, lies with implicit Western guarantees for a cordon of vigorous nation-states along her eastern and southern frontiers. Such a development is not soon likely; but the transformation of the world balance of power is, in the long run, no more favorable to China than to any other aggressive state. The Japanese will assert themselves again within the decade—indeed, they are already doing so, as we Americans have occasion to know. At present they assert a kind of militant pacifism in which it is not difficult to detect an element of provocation against their conquerors and occupiers who now would wish undone the reversal of values instituted at the war's close. But this speaks of a renewed national sense of self-reliance which is the best America can wish for Japan.

In time too Indian power will grow: particularly if sizable capital funds are made available to finance her "take-off" into the industrial age. Even today India ought not to be underestimated as a military power entrenched behind a mountain barrier. The approaching diminution of her rivalry with Pakistan, a development facilitated by the Chinese probes into the Himalayan frontier regions, frees her to deploy these forces against the giant to the north. There is a fashion in the West to discount India; but if Chinese population is a weapon of war, so is India's. There is a modern army in India, and warrior races as well—as the Chinese might recall from the parts taken by Rajput, Sikh and Punjab infantry and the Bengal Lancers in the relief of Tientsin during the Boxer Rebellion.

In a sense, the American task in East Asia is to undo the too-complete effects of the second World War. For if America could not permit the Japanese Empire hegemony over the Western Pacific and the East Asian mainland, it is no less unreal for America to expect Japan to remain forever in national impotence. The suppression of Japanese power and the absence of more than putative power in India have created a vacuum in East and South Asia which tempts the Chinese to folly. Yet a triangle of powerful states in this region, in which no single nation could exert a decisive superiority over a combination of the other two, could provide the best long-range prospect for stability in Asia.

CHAPTER SIX

The New Nations

And what now develops, in the space of hardly a century, is a drama of such greatness that the men of a future Culture, with other souls and other passions, will hardly be able to resist the conviction that "in those days" nature herself was tottering. The politics stride over cities and peoples; even the economics, deeply as they bite into the destinies of the plant and animal worlds, merely touch the fringe of life and efface themselves. But this [industrial] technique will leave traces of its heyday behind it when all else is lost and forgotten. For this Faustian passion has altered the Face of the Earth.

—Oswald Spengler

HISTORIANS MAY label our times the century of the crisis of European civilization, but the events that have convulsed Europe in the last sixty years—the fratricidal wars of nationalism and ideology—are the climax of forces set loose in the nineteenth century. So too is the spread to Asia and Africa of industrial civilization and Western modes of thought, though again it is only in this century that we have begun to reap the whirlwind.

The revolutionary consequences of this movement are already apparent in parts of Asia; the conversion of Africa to a self-sustaining industrial civilization lies in the future. But what is also yet to come is the transformation of the distribution of global power. For the sway now held over world affairs by Russia, America, and Europe can only be weakened with time, while new powers arise with the ability to enforce their decisions.

As nationalism and technology kindle the dry societies of Asia and Africa, it is possible dimly to see something like the old seventeenth-century world emerging. In that pre-industrial age Europe, brilliant, restless, seeking, still shared dominion with the Osmanlis, the Moghuls, the serene empire of the Ch'ings. One by one the Asian empires faltered; today their descendants are quickening as the Industrial Revolution, which gave Europe its suzerainty, reaches them.

The character of the years to come will, in large measure, be shaped by these new and reawakened regions. As Arnold Toynbee has noted:

Future historians will say, I think, that the great event of the twentieth century was the impact of the Western civilization upon all the other living societies of the world of that day. They will say of this impact that it was so powerful and so pervasive that it turned the lives of all its victims upside down and inside out.... This will be said, I feel sure, by historians looking back on our times even from as short a time hence as A.D. 2047.... [But] the historians of A.D. 3047 ... may have something far more interesting ... to say ... [They] will, I believe, be chiefly interested in the tremendous coun- ter-effects which, by that time, the victims will have produced in the lives of the aggressor. By [then] our Western civilization, as we and our Western predecessors have known it, say, for the last twelve or thirteen hundred years, since its emergence out of the Dark Ages, may have been transformed, almost out of all recognition, by a counter-radiation of influences from the foreign worlds which we, in our day, are in the act of engulfing in ours....[1]

But there is no need to discount the vigor of Europe to acknowledge the importance of the return to politics of civiliza- tions which for three hundred years have been silent, nor of Africa's galvanic entrance into historical time. It would be a mistake to discount Europe; it has been the most resourceful of civilizations; and there is no proof that its vigor is spent. What must be acknowledged is that Africa and Asia will not slavishly imitate Europe. For if Russian Communism has been, in a sense, the reaction of a quasi-European nation and culture to the encroachment of Western industrialism and ideology, we must expect reactions at least equally bizarre from cultures more alien still.

Inchoate as the future of the non-European world may be, in the present chapter we shall try first of all to single out a few—very few—of the significant forces at work in North Asia, in India, in the Islamic states, in Latin America, and then in the separate crucible of Africa, in an effort to identify some of the elements which we may expect to interact with Western material techniques and ideologies. Finally we may narrow the focus to the specific roles Communism, a variant Western ideology, has thus far played in two Asian states and thereby estimate its probable future in these regions.

Asia today is preoccupied, perhaps obsessed, with the material components of European civilization; but perhaps more important than the impact of Western technology on Asia are the consequences of introducing into Asian cultures that intellectual force which has made technology possible. For modern technology and the European ethos are closely intertwined, though Asians have not always been willing to acknowledge the connection. We may profoundly respect Asia; we may acknowledge the shadowy existence of African tribal empires in pre-industrial centuries—Mandingo and Songhoy—but it is Europe that has produced Newton and Galileo, Leibnitz and Harvey, Pasteur, Nils Bohr, Freud, and Einstein. Europe since the Greeks has been conscious of a *worldly* mission. Redemption of the time has been a meaningful phrase in Europe, whereas, Islam apart, the great introspective cultures of Asia have tended to seek escape from time and worldly demands, the extinction of desire. Europe has recognized a political destiny, a linear history with a beginning, a movement, and an end. In Asia history has been regarded as circular, human victory consisting in a transcending of history rather than a fulfillment of it.

The West has been permanently concerned with reconciling

the temporal and the eternal. The Greeks expressed the human implication in time with the Promethean myth; and Judaism and Christianity—and Islam—are religions embedded in history, regarding man's fate as bound up in a corporate adventure in time. Christianity's Redeemer was God incarnate in man; the world could never be abjured after such an event. Essential to this view has been the Western understanding of human freedom: that man's autonomy has not, as with animals, the character of a datum—sufficing that they are what they are for their tendencies to conform with their law. Men are seen as enjoying a terrible liberation from this necessity and an original capacity to choose among possibilities, to see a purpose to their actions. Camus has written: "There is but one truly serious philosophical problem, and that is suicide. Judging whether life is or is not worth living amounts to answering the fundamental question of philosophy." He goes on: "The world in itself is not reasonable, that is all that can be said. But what is absurd is the confrontation of this irrational and the wild longing for clarity whose call echoes in the human heart." [2] He was formulating the central question of Western philosophy, how the transcendent and the mundane are to be reconciled. His conclusion: the paradox acknowledged, "the point is to live"; and it is the answer to which the West has always returned.

But Asia has answered the question in other ways—the world is to be endured and escaped. This is the Lord Gautama, after Enlightenment, to his five disciples in the deer park at Benares:

These two ends, almsmen, are not to be followed by one-who-has-left-the-world. Which two? That which is clinging addiction to the will-to-welfare . . . and that which is addiction to the tormenting of the self. Now by the Wayfarer not having gone up to either of these ends, a middle course has been thoroughly understood, making vision, making knowledge, which conduces to calm after toil . . . to nirvana. . . . This now, almsmen, is the origin [of wrongful things]: that which is craving, rebecoming-ish, accompanied by pleasure and passion, finding delight here and there, namely craving for will to sensuous welfare, craving for becoming, craving for prosperity. But

this now, almsmen, is [the ending of ill things]: the fading out and
ending of just that craving, giving up, surrender, release....[3]

Thus it is hardly surprising that neither Hinduism nor Buddhism
has developed a political philosophy.

In North Asia, less *serious* about philosophy, there has been
by contrast a politics—witness the cold-blooded maxims of the
Realists, advisers to the Ch'in Emperors:

> Now, former kings were able to make their people tread on naked
> swords, face showers of arrows and stones. Was it that the people
> liked doing it? Not at all; but they had learnt that by doing so they
> escaped from even worse harm. Therefore I would have the people
> told that if they want gain, it is only by ploughing that they can get
> it; if they fear harm, it will only be by fighting that they can escape it.

And they go on:

> The enlightened ruler lets the Law choose men; he does not find
> them himself. He lets the Law weigh achievements; he does not
> measure them himself.... Those who show capacity for their work
> and carry out what they have promised are rewarded; those who
> show incapacity and do not carry out what they promised are
> punished.... Those who promise little and perform much are also
> punished. Not that the ruler is not pleased at what they have done;
> but he knows that the harm of "words" not fitting "realities" is
> greater than the gain of even the highest achievement. That is why
> he punishes.[4]

But Chinese philosophy—and Japanese—has never committed
itself to a teleology; there is no conviction of progress, no working out of *ends*. For North Asia history, if not cyclical, is a
descent; the aim of philosophy and politics is to establish a
fundamental harmony, an order of individual, family, and state
once the possession of men in a departed Golden Age and to
which mankind, if it is wise, will again find its way. Christianity
was expelled from Japan and persecuted in China after the
sixteenth century precisely because its concern for absolute
values was correctly seen as a fundamental threat to the state,

to the order of society. The ruler Hideyoshi explained to the Portuguese Viceroy of the Indies in 1591:

The good order of the government which has been established here since the beginning depends on the exact observance of the laws on which it is founded, and whose authors are [its native gods]. . . . They cannot be deviated from without involving the disappearance of the differences which ought to subsist between sovereign and subject, and of the subordination of wives to husbands, children to fathers, of vassals to lords, of servants to their masters. In a word, these laws are necessary for the maintenance of good order at home and tranquility abroad. The "Fathers of the Society" [Jesuits] as they are called, have come to these islands to teach another religion here. . . . This new law can only serve to introduce into Japan a diversity of cults prejudicial to the welfare of the state. It is for this reason that by Imperial Edict I have forbidden these foreign doctors to continue to preach their doctrine. . . .[5]

In modern times the efforts at self-defense have proved futile: the uniform fate of Japan, China, and the South Asian cultures has been to be convulsed by the introduction of industrialism and Western modes of thought. But in China and Japan the existence of a political tradition—the one of centralizing authority, the other of a feudal state—has determined the quality of their response. China's reaction to Westernism we have examined. As for Japan, her triumphal transformation of herself after the Meiji Restoration was an achievement of these forces of national consciousness and political authority. The years between 1868 and Japan's annihilation of the Imperial Russian Fleet at Tsushima in 1905 saw an assimilation of Western technology and utilitarian thought into profoundly national forms so brilliant as to obscure its essential failure. For in the years before the second World War Japan lived by a kind of cultural fiction: the forces of the modern world had undermined the intellectual foundations of the nation, yet the tradition and solidarity of this unique state persisted and were powerful enough to sustain it through the phenomenal undertaking—and ordeal—of the war. Yet the political structure which proved so tough was divided from the Japanese intellect, affected as it was by Western thought, and the repudiation of the old imperial system in 1945 merely ratified this fact.*

The American occupation imposed upon Japan a radically reversed set of values—indeed, a set of liberal values and legislation which in part would have been unacceptable to the United States. This was an experiment of audacious proportions (how audacious was probably fully understood by neither the Americans nor the Japanese); if it was so strikingly successful it was that the Japanese were themselves conscious of their failure unaided to make intellectual peace with the modern world. In a way Japan today is experiencing a second Meiji Restoration, a crisis of intellect, as it races through the varieties of Western thought as passionately as it once raced through Western technology. The student rioting at the time of the ratification of the American treaty in the summer of 1960 could thus at once have sprung from forces both pre-modern and post-modern,

---

* Evidence of this divided mind can be found in the affecting letters of Japanese university students who served in the Special Attack Corps—the *Kamikaze*. Twenty-two-year-old Ryokji Uehara wrote on the eve of the Okinawa mission in which he died: "I believe that my honor has never been greater than since having been selected as a member of the Army Special Attack Corps. But love for freedom is an essential characteristic of human beings and no one can take it away from them. I believe, as Benedetto Croce said, that although freedom seems to be oppressed at one time, it is always struggling underneath and finally will win. The authoritarian countries may rise for a short time but it is a fact that those countries will be beaten at the final moment. We see plainly a good example of this among the Axis countries in the present world war. . . . The Germany of Nazism has already lost the war. The countries of authoritarianisms are now crumbling. . . . My ambition to make my beloved country become a great empire like Great Britain is already in vain. . . . Japanese who could walk anywhere in the world, freely—that was the ideal I dreamt. Truly a friend of mine once said that the pilot of the Special Attack Corps is only an instrument. . . . He can never be understood by reasoning and might be called a 'suicider,' as he is often termed. But probably this can only be understood in a spiritual country like Japan. We, as instruments, have no right to say anything; but sincerely I would like to plead to the Japanese people to make Japan a truly great nation some day. . . . The above is what I believe without falsity and please excuse my disorderly statement. Tomorrow there will be one less liberal in the world. He may look lonely seen in the past, but he may at least himself have full satisfaction in his heart. Goodbye." 6

nationalist, anarchical, Trotskyite, apolitical, and pacifist—in all, formless and questing.

In India there was no indigenous state to mobilize a response to the Western challenge. The Moghul Empire was not a political structure but rather a foreign body itself, a superposition on a collection of polities and communities with a history of absorbing alien influences but not of acting on them politically. So a modern state was invented by the British and handed over to an elite who did not suffer the inhibitions imposed on the particularist Japanese by a continuity with the past. The problem for India was not finding a direction for the movement of state, but to find a state itself, to draw political vitality out of an essentially introspective and unpolitical culture that included a bewildering congeries of local traditions and races, and enclosed separate communities—Moslem, Hindu, Christian, Parsee, Sikh. If India succeeds, it will be as a modern secular state; the forces of Hindu communalism, most pervasive threat to the character of Nehru's Indian government, do not seem strong enough to break it, and Hinduism offers no viable political alternative. It is Hinduism's non-political character and hostility to the imperatives of activism that both hinder India's development and protect it against political absolutisms. One of Gandhi's most significant achievements was successfully to formulate a philosophy of "service to all" (*sarvodaya*) within the quietist Hindu tradition—and this innovation (due in considerable measure to the influence on Gandhi of Ruskin and Tolstoy and the New Testament) was a critical factor in the phenomenal political change wrought in India by the Congress movement.

The very weight of the Indian masses, the burgeoning of population, will threaten the perseverance of the modern Indian state, but India, in all, is the most favored of the South Asian countries, even if in Thailand and Burma, say, the man/land ratio is far more favorable. There is an inarticulate power in the masses to be drawn upon, as Gandhi and Nehru have succeeded in doing, and the elite is large and extraordinarily good. And the framework of effective national government was handed on when the British left: an excellent civil service and judiciary, a feeling for public service, an experienced and disciplined military leadership, a cosmopolitan scientific and industrial community.

The Indians and the Japanese are not nations likely to be overwhelmed by China. The reinvigorated Chinese Empire is unlikely to be any more successful than its predecessors in overcoming the powerfully nationalist Japanese; nor does the vastness and vitality of the awakened Indian subcontinent render it an easy target for imperialism. And still less vulnerable is India's political leadership, which in ability and sophistication rivals any in the Western world. Both nations, rather, are likely to find that Chinese expansionism drives their own development forward, as nations have always best defined their own purpose and identity when menaced.

There is a Chinese threat to Asia, but it is military; none of China's neighbors have found this empire so fascinating as passively to be swept into its orbit. Historically China's neighbors emerged as states precisely because they have been forced by China's overshadowing to find and assert their own identities. Had they failed, they would be part of China today. The Han have taken many races into train; and if the neighboring Burmese, Siamese, and Tibetans—to say nothing of the Indians and Japanese—survived, it was because their sense of separateness and autonomy was forceful enough to reject all but token deference to China. They might, like Tibet, have been nominally incorporated into the Empire, but they refused assimilation; they stuck in the Chinese gullet.

The smaller South Asian states are now deep in a revolution of unprecedented pace and implications. The test is whether they will succeed in becoming modern nations at all. Burma and Thailand have advantages of homogeneity; Indonesia, on the other hand, rich but ineffectual, has not even conclusive control over its own scattered islands, though it seeks to arouse an instinct for unity by preaching a crusade for the "liberation" of Melanesian New Guinea, as if a brown skin were the same as black.

South Vietnam, Laos, and Cambodia have been supported by enormous American grants in engagements far beyond their own resources or ambitions. They are brittle states, lacking even the protection Thailand is afforded by its genial political expediency. It is hard to believe that these former French colonies must not eventually evade these intense pressures, and the wrench to escape may easily bring disaster. The better hope is that, like South Korea in a comparable situation, the Vietnamese and their Cambodian and Laotian neighbors may peacefully find roles more appropriate to their needs and abilities. Cambodia and Laos have sought to do so—against American resistance. They have been victims too long—of Communism, but also of France and America.

Whatever the future of these Asian nations, it is unlikely to fit the preconceptions of Western politics. It is well to remember that while words meaningful to us must be fitted to these events if we are to relate to and understand them at all, outside our own civilization this is a linguistic impressionism. Naming something is not to define its reality, and history, anthropology, and folk wisdom itself insist on the uniqueness of cultures. If Americans of the Northern states cannot truthfully say that they *know* what motivates and moves the Southerner, nor whites of North or South properly comprehend the American Negro, still less can Americans claim comprehension of the Frenchman or Dane even, still less the Serb, the Ghegh clansman in Albania's mountains—or the Asian. Closest to us in Asia is probably the Indian, for we and the Indians, in a limited measure, share in and have shaped a common British culture. But the India of the Lord Buddha, of Vishnu and Siva, the Ramayana, of the castes and the Juggernaut, is essentially closed to us. It is the fascination and profundity of human society, and a richness of incalculable value, but a permanent rebuke to political simplifications.

Islam, Europe's sibling, remains the conundrum it has been since the explosive creation of the Arab empire in the seventh century. The nomads of the Arab island today live as they did when Mohammed was born, indifferent to the modern world which slowly tightens its ring about them. "Nomadism," Toynbee says, "is essentially a society without a history. Once launched on its annual orbit, the Nomadic horde revolves in it thereafter and might go on revolving for ever if an external force against which Nomadism is defenseless did not eventually bring the horde's movement to a standstill and its life to an end. This force is the pressure of the sedentary civilization round about. . . . The formidable environment which [the nomad] has succeeded in conquering has insidiously enslaved him." [7] Yet, unaccountably, somewhere in these Arab nomads is the passion which took them in a hundred years from a static truce with their harsh climate to a season of world dominion. " 'Farewell, Syria, and forever!' said the Emperor as he embarked for Byzantium; 'and ah! that so fair a land should be my enemy's.' " [8]

By A.D. 713, less than a century after Mohammed began his mission, the Arabs had a delegation at the Chinese court; they conquered Georgia in 727-733, and in the same ten years spent their western thrust at Tours. But then their energy was exhausted and the nomads fell back slowly to the reclusion of the desert. The Arab world which succeeded them was the world of the cultivators and townsmen—the "sedentary civilization." The Bedouin came out of the desert once again to Damascus in the first World War, and in Jordan's Hashemite kingdom hold a fragile enclave outside Arabia, but the townsmen dominate; indeed it is the Egyptians, not the Arabs, who lead the modern Middle East.

To restore Arab glory is an idea which still grips the imagination of the Middle East, but it now must take place, if it is to take place at all, by coming to terms with the modern age. Oil and Israel and relighted nationalism have changed all. And Islam itself, capable of astonishing political, scientific, and artistic feats in the years of the early caliphates, today maintains uneasy compromise with the twentieth century. Neither obsolete nor reinvigorated, it has not made peace with the essentially secular revolutionary forces of the Arab world. There have been puritan Islamic movements with political effect in our times—the Wahhabi, who consolidated Arabia under Ibn Saud in the first quarter of the century, and the Moslem Brotherhood, a hyper-nationalist and extremist force in Middle Eastern affairs since 1929—but these are zealot recrudescences, political Luddites. The predestinarianism of Islam is a formidable obstacle to political action, as is the irresponsibility induced by the fact that—unlike Judaism and Christianity—the Islamic religion has no thoroughgoing doctrine of sin or of human culpability for evil.

The Middle East, James Morris has said, a region "where high intentions are nearly always blunted, where motives are insidiously perverted over the years, where precious buds blossom into thistles, where good and bad, noble and despicable, gay and sad are inextricably confused." [9] It is the most passionate and the least ideological of places, vivacious and volatile, where politics have little to do with what, in the West, goes by that name. Even the most recognizably ideological of political groups, the Ba'th and Lebanon's Progressive Socialists, operate by communal alliance and personality rather than by marshaled argument, and the vendetta-ridden conservative and pan-Arab groups defy interpretation. If the revolutionary movements of Iraq and Egypt claim ideologies it is because the modern world expects it. Theirs are not genuine ideologies with definable political or economic theories. They are visions—grand and passionate.

The Middle East is not a backward region, except by the grossest materialist test. The truth is that it exists in a kind of relationship to Europe which is one of experience to comparative innocence, reminiscent of the interplay of Europeans and Americans in the novels of Henry James. The Levantine exhausted the conventional possibilities of guile and passionate politics long ago. The story of contemporary Western dealings with the Middle East is one of futile attempts to identify and support "reasonable" groups, that mirage of contemporary diplomacy, but the groups and individuals found have invariably proved to be either the Canutes of Arab affairs, or ultimately "unreasonable"; for the fact is that the Middle East is not "reasonable" in the European political sense. It is obsessed with itself, its own rich, erratic, violent life. It is as cynical about the earnest politics of America as it is bored by the teleological economics of Moscow. It may conquer, or be conquered, but it does not conform.

Latin America provides still another situation, for if—as in the Middle East—the hot metal of technology is being poured into a static culture, the culture is essentially European, though a peninsular one, and it has the advantage of the Mediterranean example as well as a tradition of its own. South America, in one sense, has been a backwater of a backwater, the orphaned colonial possessions of states which lost their energy, their involvement in history. As Spain and Portugal withdrew from the ordeal of modern Europe's industrial transformation, they lost their American bridgeheads; and their colonists were left to come to terms with a formidable climate and a pervasive Indian culture which—in places—was of unique sophistication. Indeed, it is the *Indian* character of much of Latin America that is today most imposing. For again it is a mistake to treat Latin America as simply one other underdeveloped area. There is economic backwardness here, and illiteracy and poverty, but Latin America is not a civilization that has failed. It is a success, more European than North America, more successful in assimilating its native population, conscious of nationality and culture, no stranger to the modern world and its ideologies.

The solutions to its vast problems of class, race, and economics are *known*.

The Latin American ethos is European, but derivative of a vivacious and unpragmatic Europe, addicted to absolute ideas and contemptuous of compromises; its political aberrations accordingly are European heresies. Thus Communism is no novelty here; heresy it may be, but it is understood. What is strange to this continent is the Soviet and Chinese ideological milieu. Latins have been Communists before, but incorrigibly *Latin* Communists, and that was in a time when Communism was in style as well as ideology an international movement—which is not true today. The old Latin flirtation with absolute political ideas prompted Koestler's remark: ". . . I seemed to understand why the Anarchist doctrine is so popular in Spain. To the Anarchists the problem of the human race is as simple as cracking nuts: just smash the hard shell of social institutions and savour the delicious kernel. A fascinating theory; but it seemed to me rather doubtful whether trees would ever bear nuts without shells." [10]

Today the hard brilliance of absolutisms has no less beauty to display; the difference is that Communism today is the diamond proved paste, and its appeal is not to the questing intellectual but to the *déclassé* and to the ambitious. Prophecy is doubtless rash, but it seems rather likely that Latin America will continue to invent its own absolutisms rather than borrow the stolid and intellectually commonplace system offered by Russia and China. If Poland and Hungary so stubbornly resist Soviet ways, will the Latin world do less?

If in Asia and the Middle East very old and subtle pre-industrial civilizations are caught up in the modern intellectual and utilitarian transformation of the world, in Africa civilization itself is being created in a fury of contending powers and pressures. It is necessary to recognize first that there is no single Africa. There are several, of widely disparate cultures and stages of development. There is Islamic Africa, not only the

Maghreb where French influence is also strong, but the crescent south and east of the Sahara which has known Arab incursions for centuries: Nigeria, the Sudan, Senegal and what was once French West Africa, and the Red Sea Coast. There is Hamitic Africa, the Africa of the "dark whites" dear to ethnologists, in Ethiopia an arrested culture of very great antiquity superimposed on tribes less touched by outside influences than any other in Africa. There are the splendid highlands of Ruanda-Urundi where the Hamitic Watutsi defend their feudal rule against the rebelliousness of their Bahutu serfs. There are the Masai nomads of Kenya, aristocratic, apolitical, hostile to change, living alongside the agrarians, ambitious, and intensely political Kikuyu. There are central African tribes stagnating in the stone age, their societies magic-ridden and full of terror. In South Africa are urban Africans who for two or more generations have lived in an industrial age and are no more capable of returning to the tribes than English Christians to the Druids. At the other extreme are Southwest African Bushmen and Hottentots, surviving, unique and precarious, at the very edge of human existence.

There are the European influences which have varied drastically from place to place. British Africa has its Oxonians and its barristers. In French Africa the French have used their astonishing talent for making another elite authentically French not only in modes of thought but in manners and intuition. In the Congo the Belgians attempted and failed at the characteristic experiment of creating a prosperous and stable bourgeoisie. Portuguese Africa—the great chunks of Angola on the west and Mozambique in the east—is little known but has a Latin indifference to race, some cruelty, and its first political stirrings. And in South Africa, races far advanced in political consciousness war obscurely with white men who profess a religion of the wrong century and cannot retreat because more than a hundred years ago they gave up any claim they might have had on another place. (There is an Afrikander tragedy as well as a Zulu one.) There is the great division between "white

Africa" where Europeans settled and established farms, and the oppressive central and west African areas where Europeans came to mine or trade but went home to Europe when they were old.

Of the whole, an analogy might be made with a Europe where a handful of moderns lived in Paris and Berlin, while in the countryside dwelt the Aurignacian hunters who made the great cave paintings of France; where pacified Teutonic tribes roamed the northern forests, while in scattered places there were feudal enclaves of the tenth century, possessing the arms and techniques of that age but no written language or speculative culture. If this is a melodramatic image, it is nonetheless useful in providing a realization of the variety of Africa; and it is useful too to illustrate Africa's potentiality not only to progress, closing the time lag, but also, should things go badly, to revert to tribalism and the somber and powerful ways interrupted by the European explorations of the last century. As Stuart Cloete pessimistically predicted for the Congo, "the leopard men and Crocodile men [to] reappear, cannibalism . . . resumed and the great Congo basin return to sleep. What is a hundred years' occupation to Africa? There have been other cultures and other civilizations that have come and gone and left no trace. . . ." [11]

It need not go that way, but neither will there be an inevitable movement toward that passionate vision of a democratic African federation often named as the African political aspiration. Tribalism is pervasive, the political divisions of Africa have little relation to the ethnic ones, and barbarism powerfully draws the more isolated and stunted peoples. Anarchy (or Balkanization) and erratic private ambitions threaten a viable political order, and throughout Africa there is the cultural malaise of the detribalized, that afflicted generation cut off from the past and overwhelmed by the present. The African elite is not to be envied. They are irrevocably removed from their own tradition, yet alien to the Europe which has indelibly marked them. Their attempt to invent a cultural synthesis of the European experience and the realities of Africa is perhaps the most imposing undertaking of any single group of men in the world today. Their determination to define and politically to assert an "African personality" was demonstrated at the eventful United Nations Assembly session in the fall of 1960. That a conscious African unity was inevitably marred by the disparate interests of regions and the competitions of leaders and new nationalisms ought not to obscure the fact that Africa —as a self-conscious entity—will bulk large in the politics of the future.

That a synthesis of European influence and African heritage is possible is evident in the remarkable men already produced in Africa. But that it is an extraordinarily risky road that Africa is irrevocably set upon has been demonstrated too, not only in the Congo, but much more powerfully—and with far more imposing significance—in Kenya's Mau Mau uprising.

Here was a movement with beginnings, so far as its beginnings can be precisely identified at all, in an anticolonial movement of conventional quality, if more than conventional bitterness. Its leader was a man of education and distinction. Jomo Kenyatta spent seventeen years in Europe, had a brilliant record as a student at the University of London, and published a notable anthropological study of his tribe, the Kikuyu: he contended that the African communal system, whatever its backwardness in technology and written culture, provided values more profound than those of the fractionalized individualism of Europe. He wrote:

When the European comes to Kikuyu country and robs the people of their land, he is taking away not only their livelihood, but the material symbol that holds family and tribe together. . . . The African is conditioned, by the cultural and social institutions of centuries, to a freedom of which Europe has little conception, and it is not in his nature to accept serfdom forever. . . .[12]

The Kikuyu nationalist movement that grew under his leadership turned, with a terrible atavism, to barbarity; a primitive

culture had been placed under a strain which it could not endure, and it sought escape in a pathological violence that had
no real objective. It is disputed whether this reversion to savagery came about with the connivance of Kenyatta or happened despite him. But it happened, and among a tribe with
better than average education and extensive contact with
civilization. It was not a political phenomenon. It was a savage
revenge not so much on white men as on change itself: destruction visited on the powers of disruption. It was something
that can happen again. If there is a mere political lesson in this
tragedy, it is that Kenyatta's brief exposure to Marxism (he
studied for a year or two in Moscow) and his London varsity
proved equally irrelevant to this atavistic Kikuyu rage.

Beside the immense color of Asia, Latin America, and Africa,
Europe and North America must seem to be monochrome cultures and their claims egocentric. They conceive themselves to
be struggling for the soul of the world, but they are wrong.
They fail to grasp the originality and incalculability of this
world. That the Asia which three centuries ago felt itself Europe's assured equal * failed to acquire technology and was
swept aside by the West does not mean that its resources are
spent. We have proof enough of this in the China which today

---

* Or assured superior; witness the message dispatched by China's Emperor
Ch'ien Lung to George III in 1793: "You, O King, live beyond the confines of
many seas; nevertheless, impelled by your humble desire to partake of the
benefits of our civilization, you have dispatched a mission respectfully bearing
your memorial. . . . I have perused your memorial; the earnest terms in which
it is couched reveal a respectful humility on your part which is highly praise-
worthy. . . . If you assert that your reverence for Our Celestial Dynasty fills you
with a desire to acquire our civilization, our ceremonies and code of laws differ
so completely from your own that, even if your envoy were able to acquire the
rudiments of our civilization, you could not possibly transplant our manners
and customs to your alien soil. Therefore, however adept the envoy might become, nothing would be gained thereby . . ."; and so on and on, concluding:
"Our Dynasty's majestic virtue has penetrated into every country under Heaven,
and kings of all nations have offered their costly tribute by land and sea. As
your Ambassador can see for himself, we possess all things. I set no value on
objects strange or ingenious, and have no use for your country's manufac-
tures." [13]

spreads apprehension in chancellories which ten years ago regarded her with pity or contempt. We see it in the India which,
as Raymond Aron has remarked, has in a sense never ceased
to be a great power. The pace of Asia's change today is too
rapid for real understanding; the vastness of these nations both
exaggerates and conceals. So we are in a measure the captives
of our own images of an iron China and a leaden India. Yet
merely to consider the military factor, India today is capable,
or nearly so, of manufacturing that talisman of national power,
the nuclear bomb; its nuclear establishment is the largest in
Asia. India operates aircraft carriers and has an army which has
fought effectively in Europe and the Middle East in both World
Wars. The heavy industrial and military abilities of Japan
hardly require comment. These are formidable civilizations. As
for Egypt, if Lawrence Durrell's remarkable *Alexandria Quartet*
has accomplished nothing else it should have reminded us that
Egypt, whatever its political talent, is a society of extraordinary
worldliness. Its curse has perhaps been an excess of sophistication.

The imposing material problems of the new states, the political ambience produced in the emerging middle classes by
their consciousness of material inferiority toward the West and
their material ambition, ought not blind us to the resources of
intellect and will in these places. The test is whether these resources can be brought to bear upon the things which make
power and prosperity in the contemporary world. These people
have in the past made philosophy and literature, and in their
time they have ruled empires; can they make machines and
administer popular government? That is the question we have
been attempting to explore.

The characteristics of nationalism in these areas are far from
uniform, but everywhere include an almost neurotic sensitivity
to foreign domination or influence. This is demonstrably as true
when Communism challenges nationalism as in the more familiar case of tensions between Asian nationalism and the West.
It is, however, a convention of Western political thought that

the nationalist concern with the Devil known blinds them to the Devil unknown. This is a half-truth. The Devil unknown has been willing to give indiscriminate support to the ambitions of the nationalists. His Western opponent has not only an imperial history to overcome, but often attempts to substitute a kind of brusque and paternalistic interventionism for the older colonialism. However warranted the military dispositions may be, the fact is that the only alien forces deployed in the Middle East, Latin America, and Asia are Western forces. And again, whatever the reasons, these forces have acted—in Indochina and Algeria, Korea and Malaya, Lebanon, Guatemala, Jordan, and Suez.

Western policy has implacably sought the formal alignment of nationalist governments with the Western cause. The choice for most of these governments, then, has been simple enough. Convinced that their interests are served by non-alignment, they have resisted the West and accepted the support of a Russia which seemingly asked nothing. That it *has* asked nothing is the crucial fact. No matter how true it may be that the Soviets expect eventually to demand a very great deal indeed, their policy since the mid-1950's has been to endorse and support the non-alignment policies of the nationalist governments. This has given the Soviet Union a general, although by no means invariable, diplomatic ascendancy over the Western powers in the new nations. The United States, by a kind of superstitious awe for the claims of Marxist predestinarianism, has interpreted this ascendancy as a successful campaign in the struggle for the world, and as a series of true defeats of Western hopes. Yet the Soviets and the Americans are both captives of their own fantasies. The fact is that Russia has not won a single conclusive victory in the underdeveloped world; it has only associated itself with the victories of nationalism. And ironically, the Chinese are the only people who have pointed this out. The Russians have been compelled to defend themselves against the Chinese criticisms, rejoining that non-Communist nationalist movements "breach the imperialist front" and that only "leftists and hopeless dogmatists" would disparage the policy of supporting nationalism. To insist on exporting revolution, the Soviets say, is to indulge in "a most dangerous form of sectarianism, leading to self-isolation." [14]

The Soviets argue that Communism will follow the nationalist revolutions in due course. But this confidence in the workings of Marxist history is supported by nothing in the record of Afro-Asian and Latin American nationalism since the war. Indeed, the evidence is all in the other direction. Communism's only permanent success since 1950 was in Indochina where, beginning as a part of an authentic nationalist rebellion against French control, it had after eight years of colonial war gained thorough military control over North Vietnam and over the nationalist movement which, had it not accepted Communist tutelage, would have had to surrender to the French. Everywhere else in Asia, Communist military and subversive action has ignominiously failed: in Burma, in Indonesia, in Malaya, in the Philippines, in India's Hyderabad state—in every place where nationalism has been able to find expression in authentic governments or genuine political movements, and was not compelled, by war, into fatal dependence upon the material support the Communists could provide from abroad.

The Communists have been no luckier in their political competitions within these new nations. They have had successes —in Indonesia, in India—so long as they have put nationalism first, but each time they have stopped behaving like nationalists and have begun behaving like Communists they have come into conflict with nationalism, and they have been defeated.

It is worth examining in some detail the two instances in which the Communists have made the most significant bids for power. A third, Cuba, at this writing the most dramatic example of the alliance between Communism and nationalism, provides enough originality to warrant separate treatment.

Kerala State in India elected a Communist government in 1957. It was the first time in history that the Communists had won power by parliamentary means, and their success had the greatest significance both for the Indian Communist Party (long torn between Left and Right factions, one advocating violence and other parliamentary action) and for India itself. There was talk that Kerala could prove the Yenan of India.

The Communists had taken a minority of the popular vote (35%) but were the single largest party in the legislature and with the support of several independents securely controlled the house. The Communists had come to power as a reform force in a state which was experiencing notoriously corrupt and inefficient government and where communal hostilities were serious. The Communists assumed office with the public weary of discord and anxious for effective government, generally disposed to expect the best of the new administration.

Twenty-eight months later the President of India took over control of the state and dissolved the Communist administration on grounds that constitutional government in Kerala had broken down. A popular movement allying Hindus, Moslems, Christians, the Congress Party, the Praja Socialists, the Revolutionary Socialists, and the Muslim League had by mass action of unprecedented scale forced the central government to intervene against an administration which refused to resign and was using violence to put down resistance. Slowly accruing resentments had culminated in a month and a half of anti-Communist mass demonstrations larger than the demonstrations of the days of India's independence struggle.

The sympathy which the Communists commanded when they took office had been squandered because the Communists had inevitably behaved like Communists. They had studied the textbook: they had attempted to gain political control over the private schools, the civil service, and the administration of the police. "Popular forces" had been encouraged to supplant constitutional government. Extra-legal "people's courts" had been created and Communist groups in the villages and towns encouraged in violence. The Party had attempted to create a state within the state. But the result of these efforts was no day-by-day fragmenting of the opposition. *The Economist* reported:

Two years of Communist rule brought about a non-Communist unity that nothing else [had] been able to achieve. From ... [the] upheaval which forced presidential intervention, a young, active and sanguine Congress Party has emerged. ... In India today Kerala alone has a Congress Party organization reminiscent of the heroic days of the independence movement.[15]

The case of Iraq is even more significant, for here there was a bloody and ill-managed nationalist revolution followed by a period of hysterical and erratic government—a period during which the vigorous Iraqi Communist Party (which in 1956 had at most 5,000 members) was singled out by the government for official favor. By mid-1959, after a half year of revolutionary rule, it seemed that the great prize of Iraq, with all its resources of oil and strategy, commanding the land routes from the Mediterranean to the East and from Russia to Suez and Africa, lay vulnerable to any group disciplined and ruthless enough to take it.

As the sixth month of the revolution passed, the Communists seemed that group. Their friends at the highest levels included the aide-de-camp to General Kassem, the President of the "People's Court," and the Military Prosecutor. They had successfully infiltrated the security forces, and those forces had been used to destroy rival groups. Communist units in the militia and the Communist-controlled paramilitary "peace partisans" had a formidable potential for insurrection. There was significant Kurdish tribal support for the Communists. The streets were theirs; "the Communists had driven rival gangs off the streets and ... they, and they alone, could mobilize mob savagery as an instrument of entanglement and even assault. ... They controlled the purge committees in government departments and the committees of the professional, the teachers', and the students' associations. ... Disposing in this way of the power of appointment and reward, of boycott or dismissal, they could regulate the country's intellectual and professional life. The victims of this inquisition could be mauled or murdered by the P.R.F. [Popular Resistance Forces—the militia] or saved for an outburst of the mob. . . ." [16] The official censorship, propaganda, and broadcasting offices reflected Communist policies (sometimes, as in the case of Baghdad Radio, in conflict with government policy). Only Chinese and Soviet news agencies were allowed to operate and anti-Communist presses had been destroyed.

Yet the Communists failed. The time came when their interests collided with the interests and rivalries of Arab nationalism, and they were thrown aside. By smashing their rivals in Iraq, the Communists had attempted to gain predominant power in that country; by building up General Kassem and an Iraqi revolutionary government allied with the Communist Party, they had expected to create in Baghdad a nationalist center powerful enough to challenge Cairo. They were defeated by both Kassem and Cairo.

General Kassem had been willing to allow his Communist supporters to overrun his other domestic rivals, but he proved quite unwilling to allow the Communists to enter his government or long to remain the single organized political force in Iraq. Nor was President Nasser (who had always seen the Egytian and Syrian Communists as a threat to his own regime and had suppressed them) willing to tolerate a nationalist-Communist challenge from Iraq. In December 1958 Nasser began an attack on the Iraqi and exiled Syrian Communists, and by April he was—despite his good relations with the Soviet Union—alleging that there existed "a basic Communist plan to take over Iraq . . . [to be] followed by destruction of unity between Syria and Egypt. The final Communist aim [is] to establish a 'red' fertile crescent composed of Iraq, Syria, Jordan, Lebanon and Kuwait. . . . I unmasked this conspiracy against the Arab people. . . . Baghdad . . . has now become the headquarters of international Arab Communism." [17] This flamboyant propaganda was accompanied by a drastic reorganization of the administration of the Syrian region of the UAR and an ambitious three-year development plan to secure Syria against the pull of neighboring Iraq. There was offensive action too, and the Egyptians gave arms and equipment to the abortive Mosul rebellion against the Kassem government.

General Kassem simultaneously was finding himself to be alone in Baghdad with the Communists—all the other political groups wrecked or rendered helpless. At the end of April 1959 the Communists confidently demanded a place in the Iraqi government. Kassem refused. Not only was he unwilling to give them office, but he set about checking their power. During the months that followed, the government slowly undermined the Communists. The following January licenses were offered for a renewal of political party activity in the country. The licenses were given to the several groups which would support Kassem —and to a splinter faction of Communists disloyal to Moscow. When the astonished main body of the Communists demanded a license they were rejected—there could hardly be two licensed Communist parties. Since then anti-Communist groups have been permitted to re-form, newspapers have been allowed to attack Communism, and the government press and radio have tempered their enthusiasm for the Soviet Union and the Soviet bloc nations.

It had been a characteristic episode in a story which may be expected to continue in the Arab world and elsewhere. The local Communists, allied with a reform or revolutionary movement, enjoyed spectacular influence and prestige until they came to pose a threat to local interests and the revolution itself. By mobilizing extra-legal forces—the street demonstrators and armed "peace partisans," by sponsoring "people's courts" and seizing political control in unions, associations, and government bureaus—they came to threaten the organization and structure of the state itself. The state defended itself. In Iraq, as elsewhere, the revolutionary government wished to avoid open conflict with the Communists, preferring to keep this powerful but dangerous force to use against other possible enemies. The task was to control it without being compelled to kill it. In the Iraq of General Kassem in the winter of 1960 it appeared that the controls imposed on Communism were effective.

As for the Communists' own plans, unlike their allies in Eastern Europe fifteen years earlier they had no occupying or encircling Soviet army to put them into power. They had to play the political game like everyone else, only with a singular and powerful handicap: their ultimate allegiance, as everyone knew, was to a force outside Iraq and outside the Arab world. Colonel Nasser had ruthlessly used this fact against them, so forcibly that Soviet Premier Khrushchev himself had, at the 21st Congress of the Soviet Communist Party in early 1959, been provoked to deny certain charges that Communists weakened and divided the struggle against imperialism. Nasser replied on March 30, 1959: "Those who talk of democracy should remember what happened to their country in 1917, when parliament was dismissed by force of arms. Now they forget their history and their chief stands up and attempts to stir up feelings against us—but no President of any foreign state can cause dissension among us and split our nation. We will not be subjected—either by West or East." [18] It was a fitting statement of what had happened—in Cairo, but also in rival Baghdad.

For the fact of the matter is that these are not "uncommitted" nations. They are profoundly committed—to their own interests as they conceive their interests: to autonomy, nationalism, and national fulfillment. Their self-absorption, their individual vitality and distinctive vision, prevent them from easy conformation to the stereotypes of Communism—or to any other facile predictions of outsiders.

The prodigious transformation now taking place in the Southern Hemisphere will bring original horrors as well as triumphs. There is potentiality here for despotisms of entirely new kinds, for yet other mixtures of militarism, terror, and debased philosophy; for pan-racial movements or xenophobic tyrannies. We need to acknowledge that a mere forty years of European totalitarianisms has not exhausted the gothic possibilities of history.

The West in general, and the United States in particular, can and should attempt to influence this transformation, to put upon it the mark of their best accomplishments; the doctrine of progress does have a meaning in the passing from one generation to the next, and from one society to another, the accruing accomplishments of history. But the Western political approach to this changing world can only be fruitful if we shake off the myths which since 1945 have obsessed our political imaginations.

One may see something of the dismaying possibilities of the future in what is happening in Cuba as well as in what has already happened in Iraq. If we are looking for novel forms of despotism, we may discern them here. It is as dangerous as it is delusory to attempt to interpret these happenings by the procrustean categories of Communist subversion. There are quite new qualities to both these nationalist revolutions and they may presage other revolutions of the future.

The revolutionary governments of Iraq and Cuba have made a novel mixture of certain European totalitarian techniques with native elements. Both governments are profoundly non-ideological, lacking any coherent view of politics and economics as disciplines. Unlike Fascism and Communism they have not even the pretensions of science or philosophy. Their claimed ideologies are patches and tatters of Socialist technique, Marxist revolutionary cant, and Western progressivism. They exalt a nationalism that has no intellectual content and is rather an emotion that veers into hopeless excess. They are impatient and intolerant and singularly unpragmatic, set on remaking society by sheer assault. They are contemptuous of experience and method and are convinced that energy can serve for knowledge. Their passion to metamorphosize their societies is profoundly decent; it is not to be despised by the rich and complacent; but it is dangerous because it is incompetent.

The style of these governments is hysteria. Lacking, as they do, realizable political and economic programs, insecure, menaced by counterrevolution, regional rivalries, and the pressures of the Cold War, they resort to propaganda and the manipulation of mass emotions to keep political momentum. Mass movements, "popular forces," an incessant barrage of domestic propaganda—the whole apparatus of television marathons, public demonstrations and trials, and symbolic villains and heroes—have a fundamental role in their quest for legitimacy.

Elevated to places of exaggerated world importance by the contentions of the Cold War, they enthusiastically join in, interpreting their private experience as part of vast world movements and seeking to export their own revolutions. They see themselves as part of history writ large.

Such disciplined forces as the Communist Party work initially with great advantages in these disrupted states, and when the Soviet Union and China provide diplomatic support to the revolutionary governments the local Communists enjoy prestige as well as opportunity. Yet these short-term advantages in the volatile and passionate atmosphere of the revolutionary regimes work to the eventual disadvantage of the Communists. They must impose their social and cultural straitjacket on these manic states. The example of Iraq indicates that these regimes will not willingly submit to the rigidities of Communism, nor, when these states are remote from Communist borders, are the leaders of international Communism likely to wish to incur responsibilities that they have not the military ability to enforce. To sponsor disorder is one thing; to impose an imperial government is another.

But the examples of Cuba and Iraq—and Peròn's Argentina and revolutionary Egypt, where this kind of politics was foreshadowed—suggest that this phenomenon is likely to spread elsewhere in the world. It is a kind of government peculiarly appropriate to an immature people liberated after years of debasement, frustrated and, in considerable degree, impotent. Like passionate men denied fulfillment of their ambition, these states seek release in fantasies of persecution and triumph. We are especially likely to see other such regimes in Africa; indeed the first months of Congolese independence gave us an even more terrifying version of Cuban tactics.

So Cuba is not a phenomenon of the past but of the future. It is an original, and there will be others to come, as all of this Southern Hemisphere, drawn from a sleep of three centuries, searches for the treasures of technical accomplishment and national identity.

CHAPTER SEVEN

Nuclear Weapons

> *Then I went down to the potter's house, and, behold, he wrought a work upon the wheels. And the vessel that he made of clay was marred in the hand of the potter: so he made it again another vessel, as seemed good to the potter to make it.*
>
> —*Jeremiah, XVIII, v. 3-5*

WE HAVE examined the general course of events in Russia, China, and the new states of the Southern Hemisphere. We have seen that events in these three areas are not, in the perspective of history, entirely unique—their significance can best be read in terms of the past, though admittedly the past will not tell the whole story. It remains now to consider the special role of the technology of war as it affects the emerging power balance in the world. And here we come up against a problem different in kind. The technology of nuclear weapons and modern delivery systems is something qualitatively new: there are only the most marginal historical parallels to these weapons and means of delivery. For the first time the *offensive* has won a victory over the *defensive* of truly decisive proportions. Therefore in discussing the influence of nuclear technology on international affairs, we would be wise to let our imaginations loose. For mankind as a whole is on the ascending slope of a logarithmic curve of technology: the next fifty years will see swifter technical change than the two-hundred-odd years since the first stirrings of the Industrial Revolution in the England of the Hanover kings.

The first point that needs stressing is that we are not dealing with a mere *quantum* change in affairs. When the first atom bombs were dropped on Hiroshima and Nagasaki, in August 1945, the assertion was quickly made—and so often made as to become banal—that mankind was entering on a new age. We have gone on repeating the assertion, but we have forgotten what it means: in international affairs we have behaved as if everything, or almost everything, were more or less the same. For as Raymond Aron has noted:

> Neither in the United States nor in the Soviet Union does the deconcentration of cities seem to have been seriously broached. . . . The two states which take seriously the possibility of an atomic war, whose strategy and military policy are dominated by the nuclear weapon, act in certain respects as if they themselves did not believe in their own threats. Never have states accepted such a divorce between war preparations and social organization. . . . "Atomic incredulity," if one may coin a phrase, is perhaps the cause of this curious paradox.[1]

This atomic incredulity is all-pervasive; it affects strategic thinking, diplomacy, and even speculative thought on the future condition of mankind. It is as if the very size of a nuclear explosion—the disparity, in traditional terms, between the magnitude of the damage which can be inflicted on the one hand, and the cheapness of the weapon and the ease of the means of delivery on the other—paralyzes thought, or better, dwarfs the mind. The United States and Russia have spent millions of dollars since 1945 on strategic studies; but the simple conclusion has escaped them: the two atomic explosions over Japan in the summer of 1945 *did* usher in a new age—all our traditional categories of thought on international power and diplomacy have been, or soon will be, rendered obsolete. The diffusion of nuclear technology in the world has brought the age of the super-powers to a close: the United States and Russia have been robbed of the advantages of size. For in practical terms the difference between fire-storms raised by blockbusters and phosphorous bombs by the thousands, such as the British dropped over Hamburg, and a single thermonuclear explosion, is the difference between the finite and the infinite: the power of modern weapons approaches the absolute, the realm of unreason. The bomb over Hiroshima which appalled the world was the equivalent of 15,000 tons of TNT. By contrast the atom bombs which trigger thermonuclear explosions today have increased in power thirtyfold. The Hiroshima bomb destroyed two square miles; a modern hydrogen bomb can obliterate 200 square miles. The consequences of such power for the future of international relations are, in literal terms, quite incalculable; and we and the Russians would do well to understand.

As the age of nuclear plenty approaches, the prestige and influence of the super-powers diminish. The roster of states now capable of manufacturing atomic weapons, given the will or desire, includes Japan, Sweden, West Germany (and East), perhaps Switzerland, Norway, Italy, and India. Within a matter of years China, and quite possibly Israel, will join the nuclear "club"—if a term implying a degree of exclusiveness can then apply.

This means that the first period of the nuclear age—the polarization of power—is drawing to a close, and the second, the period of diffusion of power, is beginning. If the political understanding of our time were still not dominated by the image of the giants, the consequences of the diffusion of nuclear weaponry would be obvious. For as Raymond Aron maintained with prescience rare in 1956: "The atom bomb, developed at a moment when two states were overwhelmingly more powerful than all others, has reinforced the bipolar structure of the diplomatic field. On the other hand, once the bomb is at the disposal of every state, it will contribute to the dissolution of the structure." [2] Today the prophecy is being realized.

We must face the implications of nuclear weapons: inhibitions aside, a state possessing nuclear weapons has the power to destroy any other state, without regard for the size or conventional might of the victim, or for that matter without reference to the size or conventional might of the aggressor. It is true that a compact state like West Germany, as Mr. Khrushchev has never tired of telling the Germans, is vulnerable to a relatively few nuclear bombs; but so too is a sprawling continental state like Russia. Possessing tenuous communications and subject to strong centrifugal tendencies among its minority populations, it could be shattered by simultaneous attack on nodal communication points. The number of weapons necessary for total destruction is, in any case, virtually irrelevant to the issue. If, as the Russians maintain, eight or ten nuclear bombs are sufficient to destroy West Germany, then thirty or so would suffice to paralyze Russia—not an insuperable delivery problem. And how is the victim to be sure of the identity of the aggressor, so that he can counterattack in a last galvanic rage? We have, we know, been hard put to solve the problem of deterrence when we were sure the attack could come but from one nation alone: the problem of deterrence in the new age stuns the mind.

It is not surprising that the initial effect of nuclear weaponry on the imagination of mankind was to increase the glamor of the great nations possessing nuclear resources. And the megalomania of the great powers was flattered, for these weapons seemed suitable possessions only for the great; there came to be accepted, on a false analogy, a spurious relationship between the atomic arsenal—the size of the potential "bang"—and conventional power and wealth of the giant states. But the analogy was more than false; in its influence on foreign policy, ours and the Russians', it was pernicious. It induced a conviction of uniqueness that reinforced our own sense of ultimate political destiny.

It is true that the first atomic explosion at Almagordo was an immense achievement, possible only after the expenditure of more than two billion dollars (in then current prices) and the organization of huge numbers of researchers and scientists. For the Russians, their first atomic explosion in 1949 was an achievement of similar scale. But since then the technique has grown comparatively simpler, the sums of money to be expended smaller, the time lag between the invention of nuclear and thermonuclear devices shorter. In this sense, the progression from American nuclear monopoly, to Soviet-American duopoly, to an ultimate general understanding of the technology of atomic warfare through the world, is only a single instance, though a most convenient symbol, of the course of political affairs since 1945.

Actually the discovery of atomic weapons was prejudicial to the long-range interests of Russia and America. No more than the United States required the Hiroshima bomb to beat down Japanese resistance in the closing days of the second World War did the two great powers require these weapons, added to their already overpowering arsenals, to dominate the postwar world. But for the minor states nuclear arms are a revolutionary weapon. For like gunpowder in another age, nuclear weapons must have the ultimate result of making the small the equal of the great.

The analogy to gunpowder is worth exploring; for if nuclear weapons are different in kind from anything that has gone before, it is equally true that gunpowder, introduced into Europe in the thirteenth and fourteenth centuries, turned upside down the familiar rules and strategies of war. And for very much the same reason—the ability to wage war with cannon and musket was independent of the traditional sources of military power which had obtained in the preceding age; and the weapons themselves negated the advantages, chiefly defensive, which traditional wealth and power had placed at the disposal of an elite.

The cumbersome and costly panoply of feudal war had rested essentially on an agrarian base; the rise of the mounted warrior in armor, the *cataphractos,* had coincided with the decline of international commerce and the urban trading centers. To control land was therefore to wield power. The self-sufficient feudal manor was an adequate arsenal for feudal war: the manorial system produced the necessary surplus to feed and equip the baron's men-at-arms; its simple technology was sufficient to produce arms and armor. Thus it was not the feudal baron—or his distant prince, who exercised merely a shadowy authority—who needed gunpowder to maintain social status or hold his serfs in subjugation. Behind his earthenwork, and later stone, *motte*, the baron was supreme.

The twelfth and thirteenth centuries were the floodtide of the old military system: the barons counted for everything, the villeins, and later the rabble of the towns, for nothing. When the villeins went to war, it was with bill and pruning hook, and their fate was to be slaughtered. But all this was soon to change.*

The introduction of cannon and musket raised military power to a new pitch; but to whose advantage? Not to the advantage of the baron, surely, for the new technology of war was not an agrarian technology; it demanded skills beyond the simple arts of the manorial smithy, nor were the raw materials needed for the manufacture of black powder always ready to hand. Initially, too, the new weapons were expensive. The capital requirements were beyond the resources of the small baron, who had money neither to pay for sulphur, saltpeter, bronze, and iron in the quantity the new ordnance demanded, nor the wages of the skilled artisans who cast the cannon and mixed the charge.

* Not solely, to be sure, as a result of the gunpowder revolution in the technology of war. The decline of feudal privileges, the rebirth of commerce and town life, the emancipation of labor, the growth of centralized authority, sprang from a multitude of causes, of which the introduction of gunpowder was only one. In England, for example, the status of the foot soldier rose steadily through the two or three centuries following the battle of Hastings—a date which marked not merely the victory of Norman over Saxon, but the final victory of the mounted knight over the old Germanic axman.

The longbow, a trick learned from the Welsh, gave new utility to the dismounted warrior. Simultaneously, in what is now Switzerland and the adjoining Alpine regions of France, Italy, and Austria, there were a series of experiments, increasingly effective, in the use of the pike by yeoman infantry in broken country where mounted warriors fought at a disadvantage. Thus, even before the introduction of gunpowder, there had been a revival of interest in infantry as an adjunct to the mounted man-at-arms and a consequent rise in the infantryman's status.

Longbow, crossbow, and pike were merely early experiments in the technique of besting the mounted warrior with weapons within the reach of the common man. The introduction of gunpowder, cannon, and musket merely accelerated a trend. But it is doubtful that common foot soldiers could have obtained more than an uneasy balance with cavalry in the absence of powder and gun.

The *short-range* effect was thus to destroy the privileges of the baron, without especially increasing the status of the commoner. The chief gainer was the centralizing authority, since the king, with his wider-flung domains and perquisites, could levy, or borrow, the money to create the arms that battered down the baron's walls—and so impose the taxing authority that ultimately gave him a fiscal advantage over his adversary that was an advantage of kind and not merely of degree.

Thus far, the effects of gunpowder were to confirm the polarization of power within the society—to exalt the richest and most powerful, the prince, at the expense of the barons, the villeins, and the townsmen (except as the prince contracted an ancillary alliance with the town against the baron and to obtain new funds). But the *ultimate* effects of the gunpowder revolution were something else again. Cannon and musket, rather, ushered in the age of democracy and revolution, for with the increasing cheapness and efficiency of these weapons they gave proletarian armies new importance and new status, and ultimately the means to topple their old masters—baron *and* prince.

Without gunpowder there could have been no reforming Hussite challenge to the authority of Hapsburgs and Church. There could have been no Naseby, no Yorktown, no Valmy, no Petrograd. The Puritan revolutionaries of 1642, the American revolutionaries of 1775, the French revolutionaries of 1789, and the Russian revolutionaries of 1917 would all have met the fate of Wat Tyler, Jack Straw, Mathias Gubic, and the other proletarian rebels against medieval authority whose uniform and melancholy end was to be drawn and quartered or roasted at the stake. It is a profound aphorism that a gun is the great equalizer.

Similarly, the long-range effects of nuclear technology can only be detrimental to the American and the Russian share of power in the world. For like gunpowder war in the later Middle Ages, nuclear war in the twentieth century is equally independent of the "traditional sources, economic and social, of military power as these obtained in the preceding age." And equally, the weapons themselves tend to negate the advantages, chiefly defensive, which traditional wealth and power placed at the disposal of the giant states.

For it was not America and Russia, continental states with vast conventional resources and manpower, able to mobilize millions of men, able to produce aircraft and tanks by the tens of thousands, that needed these exotic weapons to dominate the world, though the short-range effect of possessing them was to increase their military stature. America and Russia would have dominated the world at the war's end, atomic weapons or no. Had they been wise, they would have come to agreement early to avoid the spread of these weapons; but they did not. Their penalty is to see the beginning of a time in which the very category of Great Power is negated by events.

The diffusion of nuclear power will go on unless it is arrested by a kind of weapons-control system which the world has thus far been unable to devise, let alone enforce. China, a state caught up in a kind of paroxysm of hatred, is certainly working to achieve nuclear status, and other states, as we have seen, have the present capacity, if not the will, to do the same. Alas for the prospects of such control, America, Russia, and Britain may agree to nuclear disarmament—for, as we have seen, they have an unspoken common interest in suspending the nuclear race—but that all, or even a majority, of the other present or potential nuclear powers will do so is unlikely in the extreme. The Russians and we have an interest in suspending the nuclear race; but equally the Russians—and we—have a vested interest in the maintenance of tension, if only because the capacity for war is the last refuge of sovereignty. *They* certainly can only view with suspicion the opening of Russian society to inspections from the West; but the social investment in the continuance of international tension is not theirs alone. In any case, to shortcut the profound political division between East and West and find agreement on this overriding single issue would be a diplomatic feat of epochal proportions. And as new powers achieve atomic, and ultimately thermonuclear, capability, the problems of disarmament grow by a kind of geometric progression. With the diffusion of nuclear weapons the smaller states suffer no such penalty, sheer survival aside, as do America, Russia, and even Great Britain. And here the all-pervasive nuclear incredulity works against survival. For the smaller powers, parity with the giants is a fateful appeal.

As the technology of nuclear weapons and cheap delivery systems (particularly the dispersed solid-fuel rocket) become commonplace, it is difficult to see even how such a control system might work. It is the technical problem of control as much as the political that has so afflicted negotiations—and the problem worsens almost daily.

America, Russia, and Britain may seek to exert their failing authority in one last effort to impose a universal atomic disarmament; but the more realistic prospect is the unimpeded dispersal of the means of categorical destruction. The only consolation, and it is a small consolation, is that the very enormity of these weapons has occasioned a revulsion from the idea of war. Even Stalinist Russia, a state given to every nightmare excess, drew back from the ultimate folly. Yet for a China in a virulent xenophobia, for some affronted new state in a paroxysm of outrage, to pull the nuclear lanyard at some unfixed time in the future is always a possibility. But to do so, we must understand, would be an act of total unreason; and there is no certain way in which reason may impose itself on madness. This, perhaps, is the ultimate horror. We cannot plan.

But perhaps to possess a nuclear weapon is to eat of the fruit of the tree of good and evil—to be sobered and appalled. Or, to put the proposition less extravagantly, it is conceivable that by the time a state achieves the technology and industrial plant necessary to sustain a nuclear arsenal, it already has too much to lose to risk war. The final outrage then would become unthinkable. We do not know.

We are unfortunate in that we live in an era in which the offensive has achieved a wholesale dominance; the result, in one Talmudic formulation or another, supported by the American, Russian, and British armed forces and their planning staffs, has been the adoption of the doctrine of mutual annihilation or massive retaliation. The "graduated deterrence" theories have their proponents, and even official sanction; but no nuclear power so far has behaved as if it believed that these theories were truly consonant with fact. For a state whose essential purposes are peaceful, or *civil*, the economic temptation to rely on nuclear weapons—and massive nuclear weapons —to the detriment of conventional arms is well-nigh irresistible. So slowly the Soviets have swung to the position of John Foster Dulles, which they once so vehemently affected to deplore. Announcing a troop reduction of 1,200,000 men, Premier Khrushchev told the Supreme Soviet in January 1960:

At a time when our adversaries have not yet discarded even the expression "positions of strength policy," why are we, instead of countering strength with strength, taking the course of reducing the army and navy ... ? Are we not displaying a certain carelessness with respect to the security of our country? ... The proposed reduction will in no way reduce the firepower of our armed forces, and this is the main thing. ... The Soviet Army today possesses such combat means and such firepower as no army has ever had before. I stress once again that we already have enough nuclear weapons— atomic and hydrogen—and enough rockets to deliver them to the territory of a possible aggressor, and that if some madmen should cause an attack on our state or on other socialist states, we could literally wipe the country or countries that attack us off the face of the earth.[3]

Yet for a state to rely on the nuclear arsenal as its chief means of war is an act of folly—to accept a kind of paralysis of policy. For nuclear conflict is an absurdity, in the existentialist sense; the Clausewitz doctrine of war—"a carrying out of policy with other means"—has been rendered totally obsolete because the instrument of policy is so hopelessly disproportionate to the end in view.

The ultimate result of nuclear weapons is thus to deprive

force of the utility it once had in the relations between nations, leaving atomic states with less *useful* power than they had before. It imposes new inhibitions on politics, that practical art. There are, after all, two levels of nuclear capacity: the full-scale deterrent systems which Russia and the United States possess, designed to survive an enemy attack and retaliate, and the simple ability to destroy—at whatever retaliatory cost. France today, and tomorrow, may not match Russia in weaponry; but France's nuclear bombs in obsolescent aircraft will soon be able to inflict a grievous, perhaps even a fatal wound on the Soviet Union. And Britain's V-bomber force is almost certainly of such a scale as to be able alone to obliterate the heart of Russia.

Neither Britain nor France may be able to strike after a Russian attack; but their capacity to strike first imposes inhibitions on Russian policy which cannot be underestimated.* Indeed, who will say that a Hungarian rebel government which had possessed nuclear rockets in 1956 would not have used them to prevent—or apocalyptically to revenge—Russian reconquest? The result of the spread of nuclear capability to Western Europe has been to end the military threat that existed in Stalin's time—and without reference to the American strategic deterrent. It makes little difference whether, as some Europeans still ask, America would go to war for London or Paris. The British and French would, and, in an age of thermonuclear horror, that is enough.

---

* For example, this argument of Palmiro Togliatti writing in *Pravda* in answer to Chinese proponents of war against the capitalist West: "Woe to anyone who does not understand the new nature war has acquired. . . . Since both sides have at their disposal these means of destruction, it is impossible for anyone starting a war to know beforehand the consequences to himself in any given case. . . . Let us assume that our country could be hit by the twenty or thirty nuclear charges which would suffice to cause total destruction and transform everything into desert. Would it be possible to build socialism in those conditions? We should be lying to the people if we said that one could bring socialism nearer through war. . . ." [4]

It is difficult to see how the Soviets could publish a more candid appraisal of their chances in a nuclear exchange and still cling to a shred of their old messianic convictions.

It is the Soviet vulnerability to nuclear war, now at last admitted, that has led the Russians to proclaim the doctrine of peaceful competition of the socialist and capitalist systems. The Soviets have passed beyond the point when war is thinkable as an instrument of policy, when the ephemeral prize to be snatched in Middle Europe, South Asia, or the Niger delta is worth the candle. Inhibited as they are by the threat of nuclear annihilation—a threat that hangs over us all—the Russians have sought to develop new tactics. Now it is war that they seek to wage by politics—by essentially traditional means of diplomacy, though a most tough-minded diplomacy, to be sure.

But so far, as we have seen, the new strategists have no special reason to feel encouraged. To collapse the precarious Western position in these regions has proved relatively easy; to gain them has proved to be something else. This, essentially, is the Chinese argument: the Russians have made a great noise in the world since Stalin's death, but there has been little palpable gain. The Chinese demand new and harder measures. The Chinese ideologues are implacable—but naïve. They stand under the sentence of eternity, and do not understand.

That they do not understand is the most portentous fact of our situation. And their taunting pressure on Russia, their ideological reproaches (of zealot to backslider) combined with the inevitable Soviet awakening to the futility of their present policies, may well create a situation of extraordinary danger. The Soviets may be goaded into proving that they *can* win successes, and they may miscalculate the Western response. They may again attempt to resort to that violence which has given them their only real successes.

It is not totally beyond man's capacity of reason to deal with what modern weapons have made of our affairs, though whether we will succeed remains unsure. The spectacle of the contemporary world—genuinely apprehended—is enough to reduce the mind to black terror; the reason of man seems a poor counterpoise. Yet the elements of a reasonable policy are not

unknown. Its direction would be to avoid situations in which
there is no alternative (save capitulation) to the use—by ourselves or by the Russians—of nuclear weapons. This would first
require reversal of the American military trend toward *dependence* upon these weapons. That our forces be prepared to
use nuclear arms is one thing, and very necessary; but that by
their equipment and doctrine they become incapable of fighting a major action without nuclear weapons is to court the
disaster we claim to fear. We require a *choice* of military instruments, whatever the costs in money or in men under arms.

Deeper, though, is the political requirement: that we avoid
giving specific conflicts ultimate value. Weapons are chosen
according to the issue that is at stake. If national survival is the
issue, ultimate weapons will be employed; any disaster is pref-
erable to national extinction, and that is as true for the Russians
as for us. It must be understood, as many do not understand,
that this does not require us to acquiesce in every Soviet or
Chinese demand that is enforced by a threat of nuclear war.
That way lies inevitable disaster; the old lesson of Munich
applies. Our responses to Communist challenges should be
proportioned to the issues and should leave our opponents an
alternative to simple surrender. For true victory in this struggle
will lie in checking and frustrating the Russians and the Chinese so effectively as to win that day when their megalomania
breaks itself on the rocks of a plural and vivacious world. The
true weakness would be for us to so fail in imagination and
sacrifice as to fall back on the kind of threats that we are not
really prepared to carry out. We understood this rather better
in the early years of the Cold War and we fought on the
ground in Korea, settling for a stalemate, and we made a pro-
portionate response to the Berlin Blockade. Our more recent
response to renewed Berlin provocations has been in fact a
weak one—a generalized threat to invoke nuclear war, a threat
that very likely would prove hollow.

We need perspective. Not every political crisis warrants
panic; not every seeming defeat means victory for our enemies.

We came dangerously close to war over the revolution in Iraq, yet we know now that the Communists were only marginally involved. Today we are investing in the Cuban situation a quantity of shrill emotion wholly out of proportion to the real importance of that small island's affairs. It is we, not the Communists, who give signs of failing nerves. And long ago we lost our humor. There is, after all, a kind of gothic comedy in the spectacle of America locked in political combat with Cuba.

Most of all, in this nuclear age, we need to understand that there *are* alternatives to victory—as we have interpreted victory. For to speak of victory—categorical victory—in such a struggle as ours with the Russians is to reject the meaning of history and politics and to commit our generation and our nation to the one unforgivable sin: the sin of ultimate pride—which is also the sin of despair.

Yet it must be admitted too that even if we find wisdom in our policies it may not be enough. The Communists are addicted far more than we to the apocalyptic vision, and they may make the end. Man may not prevail. But there is a virtue in decorum, even in the face of annihilation. And the next quarter century may bring means of defense as outlandish as our means of destruction. At the worst, it may be that not all of us will die; perhaps, as Arnold Toynbee has said, the pygmies in the rain forests will survive, to begin again the ascent of man.

And perhaps there is an evolutionary curse on us, the curse of mind. There is a biological thrust, we know, toward a lethal giganticism: the brainless hulk of the dinosaur plodding inexorably, in T. S. Matthews' phrase, toward the asphalt pit, is the object of our mirth. Is it possible that man's mind is a similar lethal growth? That had we been blessed as a race we might have stopped with mind enough to build a fire, to pick and choose among flints? We did not; we have been unique; for some this may provide the springs of hope, for others only a special dimension to the tragedy.

PART THREE

The World To Be Made

CHAPTER EIGHT

Policy for a Transformed World

Perhaps there is only one cardinal sin: impatience. Because of impatience we were driven out of Paradise, because of impatience we cannot return.

—Franz Kafka

VIEWED IN RETROSPECT the fifteen years past seem almost like a pointless agony. We have not been able to break up the Soviet empire; they have not subverted the West. All our exertions, the menace and strain, have produced stalemate. Now the very terms of the struggle are changed. There can be no victory, not certainly as we and the Russians once conceived it. This is disappointing, but Americans at last are irrevocably caught up in history. We will have to learn to take the long view.

The power of convention is evident still in the fact that not only we, but much of the world, remain gripped by the bipolar conception of international power. But though not all nations have quite wakened from the postwar trance, the failing influence of America—and Russia—has been manifest in a whole series of events since the decade of the fifties began.

For China has dramatically re-entered the world stage, after a futility of centuries, and by the force and radicalism of her politics shocks the Communist Establishment itself. Eastern Europe since 1956 cannot again be the passive, dark, and sullen occupation zone it was in Stalin's day. The neutral states—

India, Burma, Indonesia, the UAR, and Iraq—which once seemed such likely converts to the Soviet cult have proved unexpectedly tough-minded. We may doubt that Negro Africa and the Latin American states will prove, in the longer range, more susceptible to Soviet encroachments.

But neither can the United States preserve its old illusions intact: for as Walter Lippmann has noted:

> While in a direct and isolated and theoretical conflict with the Soviet Union, we are now the stronger, and may be able to continue to be the stronger in the missile age, our relative power over all is declining. . . . Is there any question, considering what [has happened] in Japan, in Korea, in Okinawa, in Vietnam, that our position in the Far East has deteriorated? Is there any doubt that our position is weakened in Turkey, is fragmented in Iran, is ambiguous in Pakistan? [1]

And writing about the riots in Japan that forced cancellation of the visit by President Eisenhower in the spring of 1960, Richard Rovere added:

> If there has ever been a moment of national failure and humiliation comparable to the present one, no one in this dazed capital can identify it. . . . Even after the collapse of the summit, it was possible to maintain that our weaknesses had been tactical, rather than strategic. . . . But the feeling one gets now is that the sheer accumulation of errors of application must call into question the validity of the policy itself.[2]

The validity of the policy is indeed in question: the Baghdad Alliance has been rendered an historical fiction by hostile events; SEATO is an aborted alliance—it would be possible to say that it was never truly born. Even NATO—our most genuine alliance system, and one sprung from a community of interest that transcends the merely political and military—is atrophied. Our Soviet opponent treats us with a calculated contempt; our friends avert their eyes. Our anxiety received an acknowledgment—an unsure, imprecise, but genuine acknowledgment—in the debates of our Presidential campaign in 1960. Now we know, with inchoate knowledge, that the old age is forever out, and the new must be confronted.

It was, as we have seen, a curious result of American idealism after World War II that we deprived ourselves of the convenience of hating a nation which, in terms of classic *Realpolitik,* was destined to emerge as our principal rival for power in the world. Determined to separate the Communist system which we abhorred from the Russian nation, we treated our rivalry with the *Russians* as a kind of accident, ending by largely denying the existence of a Russian complicity—a *national* interest, a *national* responsibility, even a *national* involvement—in the government we deplored.

It is worth noting that Marxist-Leninist doctrine similarly deprived the Soviets of the convenient image of a national enemy embodied in the United States. This was a penalty implicit in ideological warfare: we conceived of a world straining for unity with ours, in short for a liberation; the Soviets proclaimed a doctrine of a universally exploited proletariat, including the Americans, alienated from their leaders and similarly yearning for liberation. Perhaps too an exaggerated twentieth-century regard for the efficiency of political propaganda, the art of appealing to peoples over the heads of governments, contributed to this view.

Whatever the origins of this political divorce between enemy and system, it led in this country and Russia to strategies which were actually frequently harmful to the *national* interests as traditional diplomatists of either country would have conceived those interests to be.

Not only did we Americans deprive ourselves of a national enemy, but by a further act of abstraction we robbed ourselves even of a political government to combat. We spoke of Soviet Communism not so much as an imperial government, nor even an imperial tyranny, but as an international movement whose main characteristic was alleged to be a kind of ubiquity, whose center, by an historical accident, was located in the capital of a state which was our postwar enemy. Thus did we introduce the elements which were to delude our policies. Denying ourselves a palpable enemy, one with a habitation and a name, we moved from a contest founded in a real conflict of national and political interests into something that touched upon a situational paranoia. The enemy, being nowhere, was everywhere; and the difference between his real successes scored against us and the defeats inflicted upon us by history or implicit in the human tragedy became obscured.

The very nature of foreign policy—the mundane craft of conducting relations between one civil community and another—became confused with quasi-religious struggle for the souls of men. The fact that our opponent—who affected to despise mere politics—insisted that this was indeed a struggle for mankind provided no excuse for us. His claim to special knowledge of human destiny did not require us to conduct our own foreign policy in the vocabulary of metaphysics: to do so was to treat Communism as though it were exactly what it claimed to be—an historical force of unique quality and supra-national character.

The eventual consequence of this transcendent struggle is to destroy politics, which is incompetent to contend for the souls of men. Today the more aggressive zeal of the mid-fifties in America is fading, but the confusion persists. If the American style now is all self-doubt and questioning, and an overdue change from the naïve meliorism of the postwar years and the self-righteousness of the following decade, it still includes an unpolitical conviction that by some legerdemain affairs can be set right.

We still seek to recapture that essentially spurious influence and authority which we enjoyed in 1945. Now we question our techniques: surely if we had better propagandists, multilingual ambassadors, cleverer intelligence agents, more idealistic Point-Four technicians, all would be well. It is still antirealism—an avoidance of the infinitely more demanding task of striving for the attainable. Indeed, the latest trend is not without a rather sinister cast, for it would assume stringent national discipline in pursuit of goals which are in their essence narcissistic and vain.

It is not the Russians who have proved an effective enemy to our policies so much as time—time has rendered them obsolete, but with them Russia's policies as well. For the modulation of geopolitical terms in this emerging multicentric world is favorable to no single power. The era of giants is over. We stand on the threshold of a time in which the giant can only be a commonplace—witness China and India moving into the industrial age, witness the economy of an integrated Europe— and yet national size itself will be robbed of enduring significance by the technological progress we already experience. The great danger facing this country is not so much the old horror of Soviet victory, however much the Russians threaten to bury us, socially, if not in atomic dust. The more real danger is that we may end up a gigantic historical irrelevancy, a state with nothing significant to say to the world, of interest only to ourselves, and that not keenly.

It is not difficult to foresee such a danger; there is a peculiar evolutionary curse on the firstborn. Their fate is to be surpassed. History is full of such examples: Venice surpassed in the arts of commerce and navigation by the Portuguese, Byzantine capitalists by the Genoese, Venetians, and Florentines with their double-entry bookkeeping and their newfangled bills of exchange. We were an early convert to industrialism and an industrial society that developed in abnormally benign conditions. We are perhaps the first to enter a kind of post-industrial age, for as Gertrude Stein once put it, America is the oldest country in the world.

And our failure has been to generalize falsely from our own serene past. We have exalted parochial institutions—American forms of social and economic organization that are, in a sense, only historical accident, the products of specific time and place —into national dogma. We have conceived the end of our diplomacy to be the propagation of these institutions throughout the world—in the ancient states of Europe and in the new states of sub-Saharan Africa. Yet we ourselves stand in a kind of danger; we will have to go on evolving as a society if we are not to find ourselves, along with the lungfish, in an evolutionary cul-de-sac.

But the antidote to this parochialism is not a dogmatism which accounts for contemporary reality in terms of an ideology equally obsolete. Today it is a fashion on the Left to trumpet for Asian Socialism—that wave of the future—and on the Right to abhor it. This is to behave as if the sole test of a society and the question of its international allegiances were the balance of the private and public sectors of production, or the role assumed by the state in capital formation. This is resorting to Marx with a vengeance. For if it was Marx's lasting contribution to stress the importance of the economic factor in determining the character of a society, we ought not succumb to the simplicities of our enemies and ourselves exalt this economic factor above all others. There are not, as the modern revisionist critics of Marxism say, sufficient categories in orthodox Marxism to account for contemporary reality. The question of Asian allegiances, of the whole turn of Asian development, is a good deal more complex: the semantics are at fault. If an Asian leader like Sukarno, or an African leader like Nkrumah, proclaims his belief in Socialism, this in itself is no cause for hope in Moscow, fear in Washington, or self-assured didactics in the pages of the *New Statesman*.

For what is Socialism? If it is true that American free-enterprise theories are not likely to transplant effectively to Asia, still less to Africa, is it not similarly true that Socialism, as we commonly define it, was an equally parochial reaction to industrialism and technology in the severely limited arena of nineteenth-century Europe? And is Soviet Communism not still more a parochial movement, bearing the unmistakable stamp of the Russian past?

We are all prisoners of time and place; but to think meaning-fully about the future we will have to let our minds slip the leash. The only thing that is certain is that the future will be alien to us—and it will be alien to us whether we or the Russians "win." Nor, in any event, have we exhausted the dark resources of history with the terrors we have already known. There will be new movements coming, new horrors as yet unnamed. To believe otherwise is grossly to underestimate the past as well as the future and to undervalue, if that is the word, the perverse range of human invention. Perhaps we are unlucky. We were born to an axial age. The whole pattern of life is in flux, and the process accelerates year by year.

A nation which seeks to respond intelligently to the trans-formed world must first ask what it wants for itself. The classic answer to this sort of question has been *imperium*—to exert raw power in the world. This is the answer that Rome made, that Spain made, that Stalin's Russia and Mao's China made. It is an answer that some of our realist critics of American for-eign policy have come dangerously close to making.

But if it is *imperium,* even enlightened *imperium,* that we want, then it is worth saying two things: that as a nation which tamely watched while its nuclear monopoly was broken by the Russians, we have been behaving very oddly and inefficiently since 1945; and second, that such a policy demands a discipline of life, an austerity of national style, a political hardness which are not ours.

The international system that America put together was made for better motives than classic imperialism. That is why we have been so impatient with foreign critics of our policies. We have expected no treasure from all this; we know that of ourselves. But we have acted as though disposing of the eco-nomic accusation were everything. It is not. We are guiltier than we know, for there is nothing so unsatisfactory as the strict Marxist definition of the imperialist motive, as Schumpeter and others observed long ago. Our complex social investment in the hypertrophy of containment, this besieging of the Sino-Soviet world, is something else again, and very large.* We too have known the exhilaration of power; and on the whole, the effects have been hurtful—to ourselves as much as to anyone else. The task we reluctantly took up a decade and a half ago has indulged our taste for the merely large, our latent messianism, and our romantic distaste for the bitterness that is truth.

It has sometimes been the fate of the great ideological conflicts to end by becoming irrelevant. The passions which led Byzantines to choose death rather than submit to the Trinitarian doctrines of the Western Church subsided; the brutal religious wars of the seventeenth century were succeeded by the genteel deism of the eighteenth. The rationalist frenzy of revolutionary France persists today in a dispute over school subsidies, and Catholics and Socialists have found a tolerable life together.

This is not, as so often maintained, a matter of necessary synthesis or syncretism between the contending ideologies. The great wars of the Reformation and Counter-Reformation merely perpetuated the division of Europe on something like the

* Imperialism, says Schumpeter, necessarily carries the implication of "an aggressiveness, the true reasons for which do not lie in the aims which are temporarily being pursued; of an aggressiveness that is only kindled anew by each success; of an aggressiveness for its own sake, as reflected in such terms as 'hegemony,' 'world dominion,' and so forth. And history, in truth, shows us nations and classes—most nations furnish an example at one time or another—that seek expansion for the sake of expanding, war for the sake of fighting, victory for the sake of winning, dominion for the sake of ruling. This determination cannot be explained by any of the pretexts that bring it into action, by any of the aims for which it seems to be struggling at the time. . . . Expansion for its own sake always requires, among other things, concrete objects if it is to reach the action stage and maintain itself, but this does not constitute its meaning. Such expansion is in a sense its own 'object.' . . ." [3]

Would it be permissible, in the American postwar case, to speak of a "denatured imperialism" which invokes the phrase "world defense" instead of "world dominion," an addiction to international responsibility without the concomitant addiction to the arts of war?

terms on which they began—when it was over there was a Catholic Europe and a Protestant Europe: the two had not become one. It was simply that other matters had begun to demand the attention of men, and the contending powers, who had fought in Europe a combat in which defeat was tantamount to destruction, shifted to a vaster but less ideological and more diffuse conflict in the colonial and commercial worlds. Nor is religious war an altogether just analogy to the modern conflict over Communism. Religion, whatever its political claims, finds its warrant in the eternal, while the doctrinally materialist Communist must impose his vision on history or he has totally failed.

There has been such a shift in our lifetime. We have been living through the last paroxysm of a dying ideological age. The students rioting in the streets of Ankara, Baghdad, Havana, Tokyo—or Budapest—do not fit the old categories of Right and Left, Communist, Fascist, Nazi, black shirt, white shirt, or red. The very irrelevance of old slogans is part of the reason for our anxiety.

For Americans the first lesson in all this is time's ability to shift the scenes, to blur, to transpose events to another key. Therefore as a practical matter it is not always a foolish policy merely to buy time. Time has worked for us—in Greece, in Cyprus, in Western Europe, in Iraq, in the Soviet empire itself.

The second lesson is that since we as a nation are political and not ideological, a plural society capable of living with ambiguity and difference, there are forces in the world working in our favor.

Beyond this there are no sure lessons, no rules; a respect for the vagaries and perversity of human affairs is necessary to an intelligent and resolute policy. A new American policy would accelerate the growth of this independent national spirit, this pluralism of power which will hold the Chinese and the Russians in check more surely than our failing alliances. It would abjure our own tradition of messianism but, contenting itself with the attainable, seek to restore a dignity to American diplomatic action now lost.

A meaningful strategy—for survival, as the rhetoricians like to put it—or one which will enable us, as a nation, permanently to affect the sensibility of future generations of the world, will have to keep within our resources. Not only do our present policies commit us to a material siege along the entire periphery of the Sino-Soviet world when in such a combat the advantages lie with the power holding interior lines of communications, but we have, as a nation committed to an apocalyptic struggle, been living beyond our emotional means. The truth is that we have lost our sense of proportion; there is no precedent for this. We have had our jingoes. We have claimed continental dominion and manifest destiny, even a shadowy dominion over the hemisphere; but never before in our history have we indulged in a belief in universal competence and universal responsibility.

The American destiny, however imposing, is more modest than universal responsibility. So are our genuine needs. Our first concern is sheer survival, the conditions of security in which we can grow and flourish. This means a willingness to prevent the Soviets and the Chinese from forcing their ideological convictions to a military climax. This is not a cheap responsibility. It involves not only the nuclear deterrent, sterile in itself though the necessary shelter for politics, but also stronger conventional forces than we have now, capable of being proportioned to politically meaningful tasks. Yet while survival in this disrupted world still means military survival, it does not mean a neurotic concern with the military threat alone, nor with the imagined capacity of our enemies to subvert healthy, functioning societies. If we need to remain strong, there is an equally pressing need to disengage *psychologically* from the Russians and the Chinese.

With survival our first concern, our second is to seek a congenial order in the world. This does not mean a world in the American image: cultures are disparate and their values are unique. No nation can find fulfillment for another: it has not been America's best efforts in South Korea but those of the Koreans which have given that country its first real chance of success. Our role in Turkey has perhaps spared that country from Soviet aggression, but it was Turkish students and soldiers that gave their country a new grasp on national achievement. Nor can our influence in the internal affairs of Iran, or Laos, or Nationalist China provide those states with the orderly reform that might forestall the disorder they otherwise may one day experience—not even if our influence were invariably wise and disinterested, and it is not.

Our interest lies with the rise of independent and authentic national states capable of looking after their own affairs, responsive to their own needs and character, willing to take a responsible role (and military role if need be) in the concerns of their regions. Such states need not be allied to us, nor even especially friendly, so long as there are enough of them to assure that no single power or combination of powers can enforce dominance in the world.

Such states will serve our interests better than petty clients or reluctant allies, for they cannot be authentic, true to native genius, even responsive to that nationalism which is the dominant ideology of our century, without asserting their will to independence—without resisting the encroachment of Soviet and Chinese influences and ways.

We Americans are not, of course, morally or intellectually isolated—we cannot dismiss the world, for the world will not forget us. We prefer a world of states where the values we respect are held by others, where states are energetic and serious and thus enrich our lives and the culture we know. With such states we can have a special relationship, as for a hundred and fifty years we have had a fundamental involvement in the progress—and aberrations—of Europe and the British Commonwealth. That relationship has been neither simple nor particularly peaceful, but it has been different in kind from the relationship we have with cultures which, though we may deeply respect them, we do not really comprehend.

The American ability to influence the course of international development is very large; it is not, however, infinite. We can play midwife to the age; but we cannot exert an infallible pre-natal influence, determining, as it were, the color of the baby's eyes. We can accelerate this process of the rise to power of independent states. Rather than contract a narrow series of alliances with these nations, against the Russians or the Chinese, imposing on them the categories of our struggle with Communism, we can seek to articulate those areas of policy which we and they hold in common, without undue forcing. Further, we can seek to speed the coming of the time when, as independent nations, developed and sober nations, economically powerful, whose interest is in orderly politics, they can exert a stabilizing influence over regional affairs.

And we will do this best by seeking no mean act of reciprocity which will offend their interests, or degrade them—or us. The assumption must be—and it is by now a fair assumption well tested—that their pursuit of national goals will, by imposing blocks to Sino-Soviet expansion, serve our interests too, as these are genuinely conceived. We can seek, in short, to re-create the conditions of an international balance of power. By reopening alternatives, we can re-create the conditions in which an intelligent diplomacy can hope to succeed.

Alliances and the Military Problem: In our decade of struggle with Russia, Clausewitz has so often been quoted on the similarity between war and diplomacy that we risk ignoring the fact that there is a difference between the two. The imposing system of political-military alliances which the United States has contracted with forty-two nations on six continents is, in considerable measure, a result of this confusion between political and military imperatives. It is worth recalling what Clausewitz did in fact say: "Thus war is not merely a political act; it is a real political instrument . . . a carrying out of [policy] by other means. . . . The political view is the object, war is the means. . . ." [4] The distinction warrants emphasis, for the qualitative difference between military and diplomatic measures must be understood more clearly than we have been prone to do in a political conflict that has occasionally veered into violence.

We began our alliance program with certain specific military purposes: to provide ourselves with bases needed as forward staging areas for troops and weapons systems of limited range, and to support the military programs of states actually under threat of the Soviet Army. In Turkey, in Western Europe, in Pakistan, in the Philippines, the fact of these alliances and the presence of these bases had a steadying effect. But by the mid-1950's, we had begun to attribute to military alliances a value independent of strict military purpose—a symbolic value. We began to conceive of these alliances as meritorious in themselves, even though they had only the most marginal military justification: the alliances and military assistance programs (which usually seemed of necessity, even in backward regions, to imply jet fighters and the full panoply of modern war) contracted with certain Caribbean and other states remote from any Soviet-bloc military threat could hardly else be explained.

This development surely was part of that hypertrophy of politics by which our understanding of the conflict with Russia acquired the character of a struggle for the allegiance of mankind. But besides making ours an *inefficient* program in real political terms—contributing, as we have seen, to the snapping of the over-rigid containment ring—it was also to contribute to a certain debasement of the United States. For Machiavelli observed that any state paying over money to others—"though they may be more feeble than herself"—gives sure evidence of weakness and places itself in the position of being a tributary.[5] By investing prestige in another state—an inevitable consequence of supporting it financially—the donor, as Charles

Burton Marshall remarks, "tends to become in some degree the client." [6] It is an anomaly we have most keenly observed in our relations with Nationalist China, with the Republic of Korea, with South Vietnam, Thailand, Iraq, and Turkey, with the dictatorships of Latin America. It is an anomaly not always to be avoided; but the United States has seemed to search it out.

The alliance program, as originally conceived, served its purpose well: Russian armies were indeed contained where once they had menaced Russia's neighbors. But the time has now come when these alliances are being rendered increasingly obsolescent by advancing military technology, when they have often become political embarrassments—both to allies now healed of wartime wounds and to the United States itself. The purpose, advantages, and limitations of each of our alliances needs reconsideration.

A new American policy would thus direct its military power to those specific and closely defined tasks which are within its competence and talent. Force is a persistent element in politics, and we, in this decade, will continue to need it to inhibit and contain Soviet and Chinese military power. But we must be aware of change and accessible to new strategies.

Today we see a growing conservatism in Russia—together with that insistent ignorance and brutality of style which characterizes Communism. We see Soviet ideological innovations to justify this conservatism against the zealot Chinese. We may infer that while Russia's military threat to the world is not withdrawn, it is recognizably more rational a danger than it has been at any time since the October Revolution, certainly since Stalin's coming to power, and for that a more manageable danger. The Soviets may blunder into war by miscalculation of Western intentions or Western strength, but they are no longer a state that is likely to set out to war because of a paranoid reading of the ideological auspices. And we may recall that even under Stalin there was a profound Russian caution at work: Stalin chanced war with the United States at the time of the Berlin Blockade and again in sponsoring the Korean adventure, but he did so only when he had good reason to anticipate advantage and when he knew that, if necessary, he could limit his action or withdraw. He evacuated Iran when challenged; he ended the Berlin Blockade when it became expedient to do so; even when most outraged, by Yugoslavia's defection, he would not risk an attack in unpredictable circumstances.

China is the greater danger, and some of its ideologues seem convinced that it could profit from war. But the Chinese are limited in their military opportunities, bounded, as they are, by Russia on one side and the sea on the other. They have the possibility of moving down the Southeast Asian salient; but they are not a maritime people, and whatever their subversive interest in Japan, Indonesia, and the Philippines, they are not likely to consider them convenient military objectives. They will come into possession of nuclear weapons before long, but when they do, it will be very surprising if Japan and India do not both put aside their inhibitions and obtain equal weapons. And with Britain and America traditional naval powers in East Asian waters, the Chinese are not without powerful local opposition to any serious military action. And too, Russia's reasons for fearing a China with nuclear weapons are as good as any nation's. We may expect some desperate moments before China's revolution runs its zealot course, but China will not, as Nehru has remarked, be forever mad. And unlike the Soviet Union she does not have, in the immediate future, the potential power to threaten the world at large.

The military problem for the United States is then to maintain the desperate but necessary nuclear deterrent, and beneath that protective shield to build up the conventional forces that can be employed in a politically meaningful way—in the "limited wars" that still may be necessary not only against the Communist states but, in time, against new despotisms trying their strength against the American interest.

These enterprises require overseas bases to be sure: staging areas, supply points, air bases. But military technology is steadily reducing our dependence upon these bases. Satellites, the ICBM, Polaris, nuclear aircraft, and Skybolt provide the means for a deterrent that does not require overseas bases. And the development of new long-range aircraft, support aircraft that operate from unimproved fields, the enlargement of our air and sea transport commands and our naval forces, can provide us with limited-war abilities capable of employment where needed without excessive reliance on permanent overseas bases.

We should press forward with these developments, for wisdom would recognize that bases overseas are often political liabilities—rather than the advantageous "symbols" we like to tell ourselves they are—and actually hinder the growth of that local responsibility best able to stabilize troubled regions.

A new American policy would look toward the closing down of our overseas bases as rapidly as strict military interest permits. It would then review our alliances for their true political meaning. It would recognize the fact that any alliance is re-ratified every day of its existence, and that those with value will stand of their own strength, and those which are false are better permitted to expire in quiet. We cannot abruptly abandon states which have taken our protection, or repudiate our obligations assumed in honor; but we can avoid deluding ourselves about the significance of our alliance system. We can allow alliances to fall into proper perspective, as we are already wisely encouraging the South Korean government to reduce its military forces and turn to healing its domestic wounds.

Similarly we should stop our attempts to press reluctant allies into political engagements beyond their real strength. South Vietnam and its neighbors can never succeed as aggressive challengers of the Chinese in Asia, but protected not only by the concern of the Western powers but by the necessary interest of India and revitalized Japan, they could, like Burma, profit from domestic compromises and a certain withdrawal from the great international contest. They would be as protected from aggression then as they are now; and a certain degree of seclusion is protection too.

Momentous as is the North Atlantic Alliance as a practical expression of a real political community, its military significance has radically changed in recent years. It would be rash to hold that the Russian military threat to Europe is forever finished—we have seen in Berlin that it is not; but it would be equally foolish to continue behaving as though the military threat today is what it was in Stalin's day. And it would be equally as foolish again to go on assuming that the great issue for Europeans is whether, freed of the NATO obligation, Americans would revert to the isolationism of the 1930's. Simply to ask this question is to see its absurdity. The United States will not retreat to isolationism because it is caught up in contemporary international affairs by a subtle nexus of relations, political, military, economic, social. It will not retreat to isolation because, in the crudest terms, in an age of the ICBM, there is no place to go.

European military alliance against the Soviet Union remains a meaningful policy, but the time has come for this alliance to take on a genuinely European character and to be responsive to the changes that have taken place in the European situation.

Thus since 1956 it has been manifest that the East European satellite states are unlikely to be military assets to Russia in a European war. Czech factories cannot outweigh the strategic disadvantages of mutinous divisions and rebellious populations athwart Russian lines of communication. Nor in the missile age do these states function as a meaningful buffer zone. Moreover it has been equally apparent since 1956 that the East Europeans seek a diplomatic expression of the political individuality which they have been attempting to assert against the Soviet monolith. The Rapacki Plan, the Polish contribution to the disengagement debate, was a profoundly significant East European initiative which was broken up, not so much on Soviet intransigence, as upon the rocklike Western unwillingness to countenance any

European political arrangement alternative to that trench line dug across mid-Europe after 1945.

If East European nationalism is a reality—and it is—then the Western nations must attempt to provide the framework in which it may fulfill itself. Disengagement, denuclearization, neutralization—whatever the form, and whatever the prudent guarantees we need, it is essential that the West seek to secure a Soviet military withdrawal from Eastern Europe and to open the East European states to the fullest possible communication with Western Europe. Only when this is done can the East Europeans be encouraged in their gradual movement into societies which, while they may for a long time be Communist societies, will be accessible to the major intellectual and political currents of the modern world and, like Poland and Yugoslavia, find national forms and conditions in which their people will have tolerable lives.

The size of the opportunity for change in Europe remains to be explored with the Soviet Union. Certainly the Soviets have indicated a guarded willingness to tolerate change and nationalist growths that do not affect their primary security interests. The duty of the West must be to press hard and imaginatively for a regrouping that will ease pressures on the East European states and permit the evolutionary forces undeniably at work there to find fulfillment. This is not a matter of giving in to the demands of the East; it is a matter of Western initiative and advantage, a search well within the traditional competence of diplomacy.

The objection invariably raised to realignment in Europe is that moving American troops back from the Iron Curtain would leave Europe "at the mercy" of a Red Army which could easily strike through Eastern Europe to the West. It is difficult to believe that this argument is more than intellectual reflex, an evasion of thought. There is no reason why a realignment of forces in Europe *must* be on the worst possible terms for the West, or that such a change necessarily must involve American withdrawal from *all* of Europe, or require dispositions unfavorable to West Europe's own forces. Surely the undermanned static defense line four thousand miles long that is NATO's present deployment is an arrangement dictated by political circumstances rather than military advantage. More important still, in the words of Captain Liddell Hart, "it makes no sense that the NATO countries should continue to live in mortal fear of a nation inferior to them in population and material resources, and remain impaled on the horns of a defeat or suicide dilemma." [7] The four principal European members of NATO—Italy, France, West Germany, and the United Kingdom—are alone approximately equal in manpower and superior in resources to Russia. With the United States included, NATO has twice the manpower of Russia. Even if the East European populations are counted with Russia's, an unreal reckoning of strength on the Soviet side, NATO has an advantage of some 100,000,000.

The reluctance to review Europe's situation is not a consequence of material or strategic considerations; it is a weakness of imagination and will, a European failure as well as an American. And it courts disaster: not so much a military holocaust as a political debacle. The judgment invoked by a British critic seems singularly appropriate; he quotes the comment made on France's Maginot line defenses in the thirties by the young Colonel de Gaulle: "Such a conception of war suited the spirit of the regime. Condemned by governmental weaknesses and political cleavages to stagnation, it was bound to espouse a static system of this kind. . . ." [8]

Foreign Economic Aid. The new states of Africa and Asia, the nations of Latin America, are not likely to develop the necessary strength to sustain an independent politics, or to maintain the needed arsenal of modern war, entirely by their own resources. Or if this should be possible, there is some likelihood that they could not achieve adequate strength to fend off the Sino-Soviet challenge in time. Especially is this true in Asia, where closest to the frontiers of Chinese militarism, Japan,

India, Burma, Indonesia, and the rest know a proximate danger. In Africa and Latin America the sources of Sino-Soviet power are too far distant to be deployed with any immediate and telling effect.

The answer to this problem is quite obviously investment in the economic strength of these nations; but economic policy must take into account the question of *ends*. We are a wealthy nation, capable of exporting a massive capital surplus for use in these regions. But American resources, even granting that we have not so far begun to tax them to their limits, are not infinite.

"Economy," said Edmund Burke, "is a distributive virtue, and consists, not in saving, but in selection." [9] Beyond the claims of humanity or charity, there is no justification for foreign economic aid and technical assistance unless such a program conduces to reasonable diplomatic goals. If our aim is charity (and in some degree this must always be our aim) we ought at least to give up cloaking our intent in the offensive language of political expediency. We have our obligations to the poor and degraded; but let us not confuse these obligations with our diplomatic purpose. Such a style of language is unworthy of a great state. But to apply the lessons of the new international configuration of power, to accelerate the rise of independent centers, would be a proper goal, in contrast to the random distribution of largesse in the world.

The use of financial reserves in the furtherance of political policy is an old American tactic, congenial to the national style. In the period between the Spanish-American War and the first World War the United States, previously a debtor nation, became a kind of banker to the world, so that by 1917 America had made millions of dollars available to its allies in support of the common effort against the Central Powers. American aid to the Allies in the second World War dwarfed previous efforts: by contrast we granted the staggering sum of $33,168,000,000 to England, France, Russia, and the rest between the years 1941 and 1945. The UNRRA program, administered without special political objectives, alone accounted for $1,831,000,000.

These are sums which at the time seemed huge; they do not seem huge today. The Marshall Plan, launched in 1947, cost 33.4 billion. Since the war's end, the United States has extended 46.5 billion dollars in nonmilitary aid to nations around the world. This titanic sum must be considered with the 24.5 billion dollars in announced military aid in the same period.

In the decade and a half since the end of World War II foreign aid has come to be something of a talisman of American foreign policy, for us at home the essential distinction between a policy of American intervention in world affairs and a policy of withdrawal, of isolationism. Like so many other issues in American national life, foreign aid has been debated, and hotly debated, in terms hardly germane to the issues at hand. One effect of the Right-wing attack on interventionism was to induce on the Left and Center a kind of unreasoning allegiance to the technique of foreign aid; even among those who pass for sophisticated critics of foreign policy the *objectives* of this flood of dollars let loose on the world are hardly questioned. It passes unchallenged that the aim of this policy is "to combat international Communism" by "waging war on poverty," to bolster our friends, to win the allegiance of all mankind in the war for the mind. The only suitable comment is Louis Halle's: "Every nation is best known by its cant."

If this has been our purpose, the failure of the grand design, so bravely undertaken, is a secret we have not dared commit even to ourselves. Our distribution of funds has been very nearly indiscriminate.*

Where once we set out to restore the functioning economy

---

* To take one of the more singular examples of a lack of discrimination: Laos, a nation of two million persons, by mid-1960 had received *announced* American assistance totalling $293 million since its emergence as an independent state in 1954. This was aid on a scale of $146.50 for every individual in the country. Total American aid to India, a nation of nearly 400 million, was $1,247,000,000 during the same period, or somewhat more than three dollars per person—proportionately, two percent of the aid given Laos.

of Europe, we have come in time to distribute monies for the chief purpose of damping discord and social unrest in the world. Our general and essentially disinterested effort to palliate the world's ills would better be administered through a super-national body like the United Nations, or a regional grouping like the Colombo Plan: we would not be tempted then to confuse charity with diplomacy. Nor would our money and technical assistance be so likely to disrupt. The UN—though it is not itself beyond criticism, its own aid programs having been diffuse and sometimes weak—is a useful device in the contemporary world. As the influence of the small states grows, the United Nations comes less and less to be an institutional representation of the old polarized world. Its aid, particularly in societies and cultures where the influence of technology is still weak and the machinery of government uncertain, is less likely to corrupt the donee than unilateral programs. But the UN is a *device,* a mechanism in itself ethically neutral, significant certainly, but again not the totality of a nation's diplomacy.

As for our own politically motivated economic program, the hard core of our foreign economic policy, no reserve is large enough to sustain indefinitely an indiscriminate and purposeless discharge of funds; nor even, if one were to fall into the language of ethical pejorative, is such an indiscriminate distribution of funds a *moral* spectacle in a world distracted and in need.

Policy implies the meaningful ordering of action to an end. And this end could be, for America, not the vain pursuit of love and spurious influence, but to provide *massive* injections of capital into the two or three or four nations in the world which are, in Professor Rostow's phrase, at "take-off." By providing such massive doses of capital, and for the protracted time required, we could significantly accelerate their take-off into self-sustaining economic growth; we could re-create the conditions of international life in which American diplomacy might hope successfully to function. For our donees, rather than the petty clients we have chosen to favor with our largesse, would be those few states capable in their thrust to maturity *of affecting significantly the balance of power in the world.*

India, Brazil, eventually the United Arab Republic (if and when its policies mature) are obvious candidates for such assistance, and perhaps too a revitalized Turkey. And still again, perhaps, Poland; even by its own efforts this remarkable nation is likely to affect decisively the balance of power in East-Central Europe.

But if this were our policy, we would be wise to face squarely the implications. By definition there cannot be many such donees. A better policy would mean the end of our sterile efforts to endow the least viable of our allies with irrelevant military power and fraudulent prestige. It would mean the end of our attempts to embalm the *status quo.* Nor would it mean a policy of mean-spirited guarantees; for severed from any narrow consideration of *ad hoc* political alliance, we would not seek to ensure an unwilling political ally. Rather it would be to re-create in new circumstances the true triumphs of American economic and political policy in the postwar years—the reconstruction of Europe, the investment in Yugoslav solvency and independence. For it has not been American involvement in NATO, as we know, that has kept the Soviets from the British Channel, so much as the resurrection of Europe itself, a bulwark, social as well as military, intellectual as well as economic. And more than Greece it has been Yugoslavia which has kept Russia from a commanding position on the Adriatic.

In short, the object of such a policy would be to accelerate and influence a political process already under way—the rise of independent states, the diffusion of world power. This would be to promote the stability of international political relationships and to re-create conditions in which professional diplomacy could function—diplomacy, that is, with all its uncertainties and its demands on nerve and intelligence, but diplomacy no longer reduced to futility by the very poverty of choices open to it.

We might, for example, through such a program, look forward to a decade of the 1970's in which India and Japan, the one confident in maturing strength, the other recovered from its crisis of will and properly concerned for its place in a troubled Orient, might not only work to inhibit the expansionism of a revolutionary China but contribute to the stability of their neighbors—as India already is committed in significant degree to the safety of Burma and the Himalayan border states.

We might look forward to a Western Europe which dealt with Russia on its own terms—as it has always before dealt with Russia; to an Eastern Europe which had recovered some freedom of maneuver and where the horror was gone. Perhaps this might be a Europe able to draw Russia toward reunion with a civilization with which she has always in the past had a peripheral but profoundly meaningful relationship.

We might expect a Latin America, an Asia and Africa, still troubled and erratic, including their share of tyrannies and terror, but with their emergencies not exaggerated out of meaning, and including among themselves serious, mature, and important nations.

We might see a United States which continued to play a world part, an honorable and dignified part, committed indeed to military defense against aggression and to the succoring of the less fortunate, but no longer devoted to universal intervention and an illusory cause.

We might, in short, look forward to a decade no better than most, but perhaps no worse, and rather better than the decade now completed.

CHAPTER NINE

The Question
of National Significance

Without culture, and the relative freedom it implies, society, even when perfect, is but a jungle. This is why any authentic creation is a gift to the future.

—Albert Camus

So THE AMERICAN interest does not lie in clumsy para-empire or in the self-contradiction of ideologized democracy: the one is futile and the other a dangerous absurdity. We must remember that America is not exempted from the historical imperatives, the laws of life and decay. And the American destiny, whatever it may be, is certainly not to hold universal responsibility. It was once our mission singly to dam back the Soviets. It was a crucial role in an historical moment, played out with energy and honor. But we are maintaining that responsibility beyond its term, transforming a politics of emergency into a national obsession. We met a test posed to us, and the world is better for what we did, for the intelligence and resources spent and the lives given from among us. But we must recognize when a given movement in the music of time is ended; and when the next is ready to begin.

We must, if we are to be faithful to the truth of history, acknowledge the diversity and imponderability of human society, and search for an American national role that will be in keeping both with our limitations, and our very great talents. We need to remember that nations and cultures are unique; that they alone are capable of realizing their individual genius. Outsiders

171

may certainly help; and they may corrupt and destroy. But out-siders—aliens—cannot find for other nations fulfillment. Only Lebanese can find how Moslems, Maronites, and Druze are to make tolerable government together on their congenial blue coast; only Germans, when it comes to that, can mend a divided Germany; only Africans can make an African peace. For stran-gers, neither inventing nor exterminating a nation is a simple task: the artifice of Liberia has taken more than a century to put down the shallowest of roots, while Poland has remained incorrigibly Poland throughout a thousand years of conquest and gravestones.

It is the Soviet Union, driven by its dialectical logic, that must reduce this splendid diversity to a unity. Here it will meet its surest defeat.

For the United States, for the Western world, the choice is a simpler one. We are not a culture that has shaped itself to a single end: our fulfillment is not in a world hegemony. Nor are we an ideological culture. Dogma for its own sake is the genius of the Byzantine world; the tradition of the West is reason. It is the universe of the senses that Western man seeks to transform, not time. This is the Faustian passion: "The earthly sphere is still big enough, I find, for big actions whose success may light up the world. I feel in myself a great strength ready to be used with courage." [1] Knowing this, we may leave the apocalyptic visions to our enemy.

If our rather arrogant assumptions about the nature of his-tory and our role in it have been challenged, it is the Soviets who are fundamentally challenged. *Our* validity is not negated by a plural order; the emergence of this order is the measure of our postwar successes. But our tragedy has been to view the world through the distorting glass of obsolete dogmas, so that the rise to maturity of new states and the reassertion of inde-pendence of action by older ones have been interpreted by Americans as defeat.

For a long time now we have gone on viewing the world with an obstinate unreason, blindly resisting the breakup of the international system we put together so laboriously to contain the Russians. We are dominated by a belief that the supreme test of the United States as a nation lies in this competition with Soviet society. We have pressed the belief to the point of obsession. Yet the United States might, if it chose, ally itself for once with history. It could seek some dispassion, some humility before the inexhaustible variety of time, and perhaps turn to things which are more likely to let us put a mark on our age than an unnatural expertise at ideological warfare.

There is really no alternative. The old combat is ended; we have not won the Cold War, nor lost it, at least as that war was conceived in the beginning. Perhaps the Soviets have not yet begun to understand that their share in history is shrinking. But we Americans know that our policies are in disorder, that somehow, though we can only darkly perceive this, our society is blighted. To persist in the old apocalyptic struggle would be to invite a terrifying retribution—a sterility, a poverty of response that are the sure marks of an atrophied and dying culture. For like Philip and his Spain in another age, the effects of messianism turned in on itself are damaging:

The spiritual reverse was ... more devastating, for Philip had believed with utter conviction that he was doing God's work, waging a holy war—and God had forsaken him. There was no easy answer to this one. He and his country could turn back upon themselves, search their consciences, and, while heresy triumphed abroad, pledge themselves the more fervently to the defense at home, within the citadel, of the true faith. But the old certainty was gone, and with it the belief in a European mission. In their place came the creeping disillusion, the hypocrisy, the divorce between faith and action that were to characterize over the next century and more a Spain sadly fallen from her high estate.[2]

That divorce of spirit has already begun to appear in contemporary America. The element of hypocrisy has always been with us—as any page of Tocqueville, say, will show—but we begin to sense something more. There are the symptoms of that deep schism between the verbal standards of an optimistic foreign politics, which is the official dogma, and that awareness of impotence, perplexity, and disillusion which is only the projection onto the international scene of the all-pervasive schism between society and self at home. This subliminal awareness of futility and unreasonableness is part of the cause of our mid-century malaise.

So far the effect on ourselves; elsewhere the effect of these illusionist policies is something else. To the rest of the world we and the Russians are nations obsessed. Having sought to do the things which no peoples have been able to do—to bring history to a stop, to transmute the stuff of time—America and Russia have ended by becoming something very like the objects of the world's half-frightened contempt. We know this, though we hardly dare admit it to ourselves: we have closed our ears against the plain evidence of our senses—the foreign heads of states say it, the foreign press writes it. Not that a mature state exhibits a neurotic concern for the opinion of others—but we, the most morbidly sensitive of nations, have lost what the Declaration of Independence called a "decent respect to the opinions of mankind." For a long time now we have heard criticism merely to refute it. We have spent vast sums of money to refute it. We have affected to believe that ours was a monopoly of truth.

The tragedy of all this for America we know: the effects of a decade and a half of ideological war have been damaging . . . to ourselves. But there is a Russian tragedy too. For Russia is a great nation, a serious and an energetic nation, capable of the bitterest self-denial. They are not a self-indulgent and ignoble people; yet they are wasting themselves in the pursuit of a chimerical dream—world dominion—and dooming themselves to an agony of defeat. But this is not a tragedy which directly concerns us, except in so far as it involves the issue of our security or sheer survival. Our concern is more properly with ourselves: there is much that we need to do.

If there is any lesson in history, we ought to remember the Greeks, who

... were haunted ... by the possibilities of disaster inherent in success of every kind—in personal prosperity, in military victory, in the social triumph of civilization. They traced the mischief to an aberration of the human spirit under the shock of sudden, unexpected attainment, and they realized that both the accumulated achievement of generations and the greater promise of the future might be lost irretrievably by failure at this critical moment. "Surfeit (*koros*) breeds sin (*hubris*) when prosperity visits unbalanced minds." ... The proverb recurs. ... Its maker refrained from adding what was in his and his hearers' thoughts, that *hubris,* once engendered, breeds *ate*—the complete and certain destruction into which the sinner walks with unseeing eyes. ... The generation of Marathon forboded the social catastrophe of the Peloponnesian War, yet the shock, when it came, was beyond the powers of imagination. ... [3]

There is a warning here for us. History will not blindly repeat; but as the Greek retribution was beyond the Greek imagination so the twentieth-century retribution is beyond our power of vision to see.

The Messianic State is an old phenomenon; in this century America and Russia are the great Messianic States. They have dominated the political imagination since the end of the second World War. The sins of the Russians are legion; we know them all. Our sins have been variously catalogued, by domestic and foreign critics: to catalogue these sins is a kind of thriving industry, at which the critics grow fat. But in a sense, beyond the peculiar qualities that belong to America and Russia alone, we and they both are creatures of the age. Both of us share with the generality of contemporary states an abstraction from reality: the new international style is a penchant for absolutes, partly the result of aggressively egalitarian politics at home. Thus Tocqueville:

He who inhabits a democratic country sees around him on every hand men differing but little from one another; he cannot turn his mind to any one portion of mankind without expanding and dilating his thought till it embraces the whole. All the truths that are applicable to himself appear to him equally and similarly applicable to each of his fellow citizens and fellow men. . . . Men who live in ages of equality have a great deal of curiosity and little leisure; their life is so practical, so confused, so excited, so active, that but little time remains to them for thought. Such men are prone to general ideas. . . .[4]

What was true in the second quarter of the nineteenth century in America is still more true in those states, egalitarian by ideology, which have sprung up in the last few decades from the wreckage of the old European empires.

It is this taste for universal prescriptions which has debased politics. It is one thing to talk, as we have done, of the rise to power of sober and serious nations, states that lend stability to regional concerns, states that seek to affect those matters which they are able peculiarly to understand. The difficulty —in America, in Russia, in the new states—is that ours is a world gone a little mad; everywhere diplomacy suffers from the degradation of language and the parallel failure to sense the reasonable limits of political action.

This is the new *hubris;* for politics is not a debased philosophy, still less a secularized religion. We have always acknowledged a connection between the public and private order, but identity is not the same thing: "whether because, as in Plato, the state is the individual writ large; or because, as with Aquinas, it has a moral aim; whether it is the source of morality, as for Hobbes; guided by a moral principle, as in the utilitarians' conception; or serves as the instrumentality for morals, as the pragmatists have it."[5] That distinction exists. To wise men the difference between the area of practical action, the attainable, and the informing body of principles to which we privately adhere is a datum. This is not hypocrisy: politics, in this view, is not the art of the salvation of the soul; the element of hypocrisy enters when we deny the distinction between guiding principle and deed.

All this is not to say that we have no duty to practice politics; or that our politics must not express, so far as that is possible, the best of ourselves. If that were not so, we would damage ourselves. But politics, and diplomacy, are utilitarian arts: they merely secure for the transcendent arts—ethics, natural science, practical aesthetics and abstract, moral philosophy and the rest—the conditions in which they can grow. Politics and diplomacy are not ends in themselves, nor the pursuit of ultimates.

And a foreign politics is most meaningful as a system of defense, a guarding of a nation against encroachments. It can succeed then only so far as it addresses itself to a specific goal, limited in time, in space, in emotional dimension. A politics is an instrument; this is the thing we have failed to understand.

In 1947 we Americans took what we believed to be the Siege Perilous—no mere blunting of Soviet aggressions, but the final challenge, the confrontation of evil. We must leave this quest now. To do so may seem dismayingly like anticlimax, but to acknowledge that the Grail is not to be found in history is not defeat, but an act of assurance and wisdom.

Assurance and wisdom are the qualities we have lacked. Our generosity has not faltered in this decade. Our failure has been one of political intelligence: a slack and narcissistic materialism on the Right, a self-righteous addiction to obsolete cant on the Left. And always too there has been that unresolved tension between our private code, a hedonist self-indulgence, and the evangelical politics that was the policy we held before the world. Believing that we spoke of human dignity, we spoke only of machine comfort. The result has been a coarsening of the American quality, a debasement of the standards of public and private obligation.

It is a Marxist postulate that an economy in crisis generates an imperialist thrust; as a cure for maldistribution and class resentment it goes to war. This is exaggeration, vulgarization; but is it perhaps true that as a *culture* in crisis we have sought blindly to make of a political action—our defense against Soviet aggressions—a crusade to mend the blight of our souls? Out of disparate elements we have made a unity. There is the abiding sense of despair within us, our sense of inner alienation; there is our pain and concern for the poverty of the world; there is our own galvanic need to defend ourselves against a society and a doctrine which aim to extirpate the things we are and believe. From all of these elements we have drawn strength and passion for a political crusade at times frightening in its intensity. In our politics, light confronts dark, with the resolution of history in the balance. But of these three elements, only the last, defense, is properly a political motivation. And one of the three lies beyond the power of our contemporary politics to effect in any but the most tangential sense: this is the impulse to mend the broken world.

For industrial civilization, that society of which we are the exemplar, is infected by a malaise which our political intelligence has yet to grasp. It is what Gabriel Marcel has called the "broken world": that disintegration of relationships not only among individuals in contemporary society but between a person and his place, his earth, his past. It is what has been named alienation.

We live in a time when political thought has for more than a century been obsessed with the relationships of economic classes and the distribution of material goods. As Glenn Tinder has argued in a brilliant formulation of this whole question, the contemporary political imagination regards the great problems of human society as bringing economic and social justice to the common man. Yet, valid as this may be as a statement of the situation in impoverished non-European areas, it no longer is true in the West; it does not at all correspond to our literary and philosophical insight. Our literature is dominated by a kind of anguish which has nothing to do with economics:

In the nineteenth century, men secure within the structures of Hegelianism or aggressively confident in the tenets of positivism, men in a world without great wars and living in the expectation of endless progress, could dismiss Nietzsche as rabid and eccentric; they could ignore Melville's strange tale of an old sea captain who neglected business and chased a white whale to his own and his ship's destruction; they could remain unaware of the tortured works of Dostoevsky and Kierkegaard. These were solitary and incomprehensible cries. But they are not solitary any longer; a great many have taken them up. And they are not incomprehensible; multitudes have experienced the moods which produced them." [6]

What are the material causes we can assign to this anguish? Tinder suggests the uprooting of men from a particular place in the natural world; the replacing of a significant relationship with possessions by an increasingly external and utilitarian connection ("contemporary peoples have the use of a great many things; but there is a sense in which they own less than people have owned in most periods of history"); the breaking of an individual's bonds with past generations and his crippling inability, in contemporary circumstances, to have a reliable grasp of what the future is likely to bring ("uprooted in time, as well as in space; sundered both from the past and the future, he leads an existence which—to him—is historically meaningless").

This destruction of relationship with place and time and fellow man, intensified by the momentum of industrialism and the specialization of knowledge, provides the opportunity so powerfully grasped in our age by totalitarian movements—in Hannah Arendt's definition, those "mass organizations of atomized, isolated individuals." [7] And thus there is the totalitarian determination to eradicate all traces of the private relationships and private communities that provide refuge from the total demands of this pre-eminently modern political phenomenon.

It is, in the last analysis, a destruction of wisdom that we are experiencing—of that popular wisdom that informs a society (and without which democracy is a meaningless theory), but also of the values of craft and of the intellectual and professional life. One is reminded of Paul Goodman's remark about boys coming into adulthood in our big cities: there is no "man's work" for them to do. [8]

We need not list the ills of contemporary America, or futilely compare their numbers with the past, to know that this rootlessness, this alienation, indeed exist: we have but to ask ourselves.

It exists and pervades Western industrial society. It is not our disease only. It is not something to be cured by ambitious programs or utopian political plans. "Experience has taught us," Marcel says, "that not only are such programs doomed to failure, but what is more serious, their failure, by a sort of inevitable repercussion, worsens the situation they started from." [9] But the crisis is not divorced from politics either: "Government still is inescapably concerned with many problems bearing on the quality and ends of life; for example, with what is taught and to whom, with the bestowal of honor, and with beauty of environment." [10]

Here is the real challenge of contemporary civilization in the industrial West; and as technology sweeps southward and east from Europe and America, it will one day be the problem of Africa and Asia. We in the United States have made ourselves the industrial society without peer. Were we to find even an intimation of the cure to this power of disintegration that accompanies industrialization, we would indeed have served our time and mankind.

But we would need to shake loose from the political ideas that have engrossed us for so long, and create a new politics, a politics sensitive to the true plight of contemporary man, and humble enough to recognize its own limitations. Spiritual cures are not its province. Human community is not its to make. But what American politics might truly address itself to in this new decade is the challenge of creating the conditions in which meaningful human relationships might, by obscure and individual acts, be nourished, and community restored.

It would be easy—and by now conventional—to end a book of this sort on a note of vengeful diatribe. Americans do not deserve this; even a world that has grown to despise us knows we are better than that. We are a nation which has wanted much—and dared much, though we have failed. No people know better than we how far short we have fallen of the greatness we proclaimed for ourselves. We are amazed, and ashamed, at our failures in a complex world which we once defined in our political debates to be a simple world. What we must learn now is that our thrust as a nation in these postwar years has been wrongful: not, to be sure, in our military containment of Russia, but in the desire to make of our international politics a cure for a *civilisation manquée.*

We are left with this: there is a virtue in decorum, in an economy of the emotions. We inhabit a world of original horrors; we will have to draw back or see ourselves emotionally bankrupt before long. A certain caution in the expenditure of our passions would leave us with emotion to channel to useful ends, to the direction of the attainable. The alternative we already begin to sense; it is a creeping apathy, a paralysis of national feeling and will which is also a drawing back, but dangerous precisely because it is unacknowledged and uncontrolled.

Yet how shall an American be wise in this century? We cannot remake ourselves entire. We have our national style —and it is a style of ethical causes, exaggerated political discourse, a certain hypocrisy. "Sometimes people call me an idealist," said Woodrow Wilson. "Well, that is the way I know I am an American." We are the prisoners of our past; to argue —or plead—too extravagantly for a remaking of the national soul is to fall victim to another *hubris:* there is more than one American illusion of omnipotence. We are not whatever we choose to be. Of all nations we are least equipped to carry on a precise diplomacy, a politics which is nicely plotted, exact. We cannot do it; we had better not try; the style of our professionals too easily descends to an imperturbable fatuity. Yet we may restore a balance, a gravity which our policies and proclamations at their best have sometimes had, and now have lost.

Our ethical passion need not be false or vain or sentimental;

it includes what has been truly best in us, but only when wedded to a discipline, a certain austerity. This has distinguished our great men. We have never honored the merely powerful. We are perhaps alone among the nations in having no Napoleons, no Caesars whom we revere. Our noblest men have been the Jeffersons, the Lincolns, the Lees, the Marshalls —men whose political or military greatness was informed by a stubborn honor, by compassion. These are the resources out of which we have found our past greatness, and we may seek it there again.

For the rest we will have to search for those transcendent skills which have always eluded us. There has been an American contempt for the really fine: and yet we, who have no sense of ultimate precision, ultimate excellences, have presumed to lead the world, though we do not deserve to do so. A moral and intellectual leadership—that quality of impalpable authority which is the quality of leaders—cannot be conjured up out of nothing.

For all our ambition of the last decade and a half, we have asked too little of ourselves in everything but money. We have displayed no great ability to persevere, to endure in the pursuit of uncertain causes. Our achievements, our influence in the world, have consequently been extensive, but shallow. Most of all, they have been disproportionate to the advantages which our nation has enjoyed. Insecure in our own identity, rich yet troubled, we have taken so impoverished a view of history as to see greatness in a competition with a system which measures its own quality in ingots of steel or poods of grain. What a falling off is here: we have seized on this Russian constant and behaved as if history could demand nothing more of us than to meet this single test.

As a nation, as a culture, as a people, we will have to do more, much more, if we aspire to that kind of excellence which enables a nation to affect—permanently to affect—the sensibility of mankind. The tasks are not only those set by political struggle: they are the infinitely more demanding search for fineness of thought and fineness of technique, a way to cure the divorce between spirit and self, self and community, community and the larger world of all mankind. Thus we might hope to make a genuine mark on our times and perhaps contribute as honorably to the lives of future generations as the Americans of our nation's earliest—and poor—years contributed to those of us, Americans and others, who have followed.

We cannot do these things today: as a nation, grown flaccid and unsure, we have slashed at the best of ourselves, our roots and our tradition of reason. The United States has had a colossal draft on fortune and is not meeting it.

There is no permanent leasehold on greatness, though we have behaved as if greatness for this nation had been foreordained. Yet we have hardly been put to the test: secluded from war and anguish in our beginning years, we moved onto the stage of history in circumstances which could hardly have been more benign. We have deafened the world with our boasts, but we have known from the moment of our entry into world affairs that we have had to summon up too little of ourselves to meet these challenges.

If we are to make a greatness, to fulfill at last the hopeful prophecies of our birth, we will have to learn a humility which is also the pride of a nation: to be great in this sub-lunary sphere, as other nations before us have defined the meaning of greatness, and others that come after must go on to do. The list of such states—those that have been *crucial* to the history of man—is not so very long. England, Italy, China, Greece, have been such nations, and without them mankind must have been unalterably poorer. But Carthage, though it was powerful, was not one of these. Nor was graceful, easy Minoan Crete; nor, by contrast, Bismarck's Germany. We are not without a choice. We can strive to be great in the things that truly matter, and then we will stay free and put our mark on history. Or should we so choose, we can let the winds in, and the dust will come.

NOTES

Chapter One

The chapter-head quotation is from T. S. Eliot's "Burnt Norton," reprinted by permission.

1. Ezra Pound, "Lament of the Frontier Guard," *Comprehensive Anthology of American Poetry*, Modern Library, New York 1944.
2. Richard Hofstadter, *The American Political Tradition*, Knopf, New York 1948.
3. Quoted in Hofstadter, *op. cit.*
4. Reinhold Niebuhr, *The Irony of American History*, Scribners, New York 1952.
5. Russell Davenport and the Editors of *Fortune, USA: The Permanent Revolution*, Prentice-Hall, New York 1951.
6. Clinton Rossiter, "We Must Show the Way to Enduring Peace," and Archibald MacLeish, "We Have Purpose . . . We Know It," *The National Purpose*, Holt, Rinehart and Winston, New York 1960.

Chapter Two

The chapter-head quotation is from *The War Memoirs of Charles de Gaulle: Unity 1942–44*, Simon and Schuster, New York 1959.

1. Reinhold Niebuhr, *The Children of Light and the Children of Darkness*, Scribner Library, New York 1960.
2. Raymond Aron, *The Century of Total War*, Doubleday, New York 1954.
3. Louis J. Halle, "Has the Soviet Challenge Changed?," *The New Republic* (Washington), 22 June 1959.
4. "X" (George F. Kennan), "The Sources of Soviet Conduct," *Foreign Affairs* (New York), July 1947.
5. This quotation and those in the two paragraphs following are all from Kennan, *op. cit.*
6. Arthur Bryant, *The Age of Elegance*, Pelican, London 1958.
7. T. E. Lawrence, *Seven Pillars of Wisdom*, Doubleday, New York 1935.

Chapter Three

The chapter-head quotation is from Wallace Stevens' "Connoisseur of Chaos," *Poems*, reprinted by permission.

1. Henry A. Kissinger, "Arms Control, Inspection and Surprise Attack," *Foreign Affairs* (New York), July 1960.
2. *Ibid.*

Chapter Four

The chapter-head quotation is cited by Arnold Toynbee, "Russia's Byzantine Heritage," *Civilization on Trial*, Oxford University Press, New York 1958.

1. "Geoffrey Bailey" (pseud.), *The Conspirators*, Harpers, New York 1960; and Zbigniew K. Brzezinski, *The Permanent Purge*, Harvard, Cambridge 1956.

2. Crane Brinton, *The Anatomy of Revolution*, Vintage, New York 1957.
3. Quoted in R. N. Carew Hunt, *The Theory and Practice of Communism*, Geoffrey Bles, London 1951.

Chapter Five

The chapter-head quotation is cited by Arthur Waley, *Three Ways of Thought in Ancient China*, Doubleday, New York 1956.
1. Hugh Seton-Watson, *Neither War Nor Peace*, Praeger, New York 1960.
2. Raymond Aron, *On War*, Doubleday & Co., Inc., New York 1959.
3. René Grousset, *The Rise and Splendour of the Chinese Empire*, University of California Press, Berkeley and Los Angeles 1959.
4. Marcel Granet, *Chinese Civilization*, Barnes & Noble, New York 1930 (emphasis added).
5. Kenneth Scott Latourette, *A History of Modern China*, Pelican, London 1955.

Chapter Six

The chapter-head quotation is from Oswald Spengler, *The Decline of the West*, Knopf, New York 1928, vol. II.
1. Arnold Toynbee, *Civilization on Trial*.
2. Albert Camus, *The Myth of Sisyphus and Other Essays*, Knopf, New York 1955.
3. Adapted from the translation by Mrs. Rhys David, *A Manual of Buddhism*, as quoted by A. C. Bouquet, *Sacred Books of the World*, Pelican, London 1954.
4. Shang Tzu, 6, page 50; & Han Fei Tzu, 6, page 23; 7, page 27.
5. Quoted in Frank Gibney, *Five Gentlemen of Japan*, Farrar, Straus and Young, New York 1953.
6. Quoted in George P. Carlin, "Postscript to War," *The Commonweal* (New York), 25 December 1953.
7. Arnold Toynbee, *A Study of History* (D. C. Somervell Abridgement), Oxford, New York 1947.
8. Muhammad Tabari, *Chronicle of Prophets and Kings* (9th century A.D.), quoted in Eric Schroeder, *Muhammad's People*, Bond Wheelwright, Portland, Maine, 1955.
9. James Morris, *Islam Inflamed*, Pantheon, New York 1957.
10. Arthur Koestler, *Dialogue With Death*, Macmillan, New York.
11. Letter to *The New York Times*, 20 July 1960.
12. Jomo Kenyatta, *Facing Mount Kenya*, Secker and Warburg, London 1938.
13. A. F. Whyte, *China and Foreign Powers*, Oxford, London 1927.
14. E. Zhukov, *Pravda* (Moscow), 26 August 1960.
15. "Referendum in Kerala," *The Economist* (London), 13 February 1960.
16. "A Year of Republican Iraq," *The World Today* (London), July 1959.
17. Cairo Home Service, 18 April 1959.
18. Quoted in "The United Arab Republic and the Iraqi Challenge," *The World Today* (London), July 1960.

Chapter Seven

1. Raymond Aron, *On War*.
2. *Ibid.*

3. *Pravda* (Moscow), 15 January 1960.
4. *Pravda* (Moscow), 28 July 1960, quoted by Norman Thomas in a letter to *The New York Times,* 17 August 1960.

Chapter Eight

The chapter-head quotation is from Franz Kafka, *The Great Wall of China,* Martin Secker, London 1933.
1. Walter Lippmann, *The New York Herald Tribune,* 28 July 1960.
2. Richard H. Rovere, "Letter from Washington," *The New Yorker,* 25 June 1960.
3. Joseph Schumpeter, *Imperialism and the Social Classes,* A. M. Kelly, New York 1951.
4. Carl von Clausewitz, *On War,* E. P. Dutton, New York 1918, vol. I.
5. Niccolò Machiavelli, *Discourses on the First Ten Books of Titus Livius,* 2nd Book, Chapter XXX.
6. Charles Burton Marshall, "Alliances with Fledgling States," *Alliance Policy in the Cold War* (Edited by A. Wolfers), Johns Hopkins, Baltimore 1959.
7. B. H. Liddell Hart, *Deterrent or Defense,* Praeger, New York 1960.
8. Charles de Gaulle, *Vers l'Armée de Métier,* quoted by Patrick Lort-Phillips, "The Limitations of NATO," *The Spectator* (London), 26 August 1960.
9. Edmund Burke, *Letters to a Noble Lord,* London 1796.

Chapter Nine

The chapter-head quotation is from Albert Camus, *op. cit.*
1. J. W. Goethe, *Faust,* Part II, V.
2. William C. Atkinson, *A History of Spain and Portugal,* Pelican, London 1960.
3. Arnold Toynbee, "History," *The Legacy of Greece* (Edited by R. W. Livingstone), Oxford, London 1922.
4. Alexis de Tocqueville, *Democracy in America,* Oxford University Press, New York 1947.
5. Abraham Kaplan, "American Ethics and Public Policy," *Daedalus* (Boston), Spring 1958.
6. Glenn Tinder, "Human Estrangement and the Failure of Political Imagination," *The Review of Politics* (Notre Dame), October 1959.
7. Hannah Arendt, *The Origins of Totalitarianism,* Harcourt, Brace, New York 1951.
8. Paul Goodman, *Growing Up Absurd,* Random House, New York 1960.
9. Gabriel Marcel, *The Decline of Wisdom,* Harvill, London 1954.
10. Glenn Tinder, *op. cit.*

INDEX